Praise for *I Probably Should've Brought a Tent*

"*I Probably Should've Brought a Tent* is about traveling with honesty, beauty, and awkwardness. Erik takes into account where his adventures fall in a long history of human conflict and shifting landscapes. He ventures out to these wild and majestic sites, all the while keeping integrity and humor close."

—Teresa Lynn Hasan-Kerr, travel writer for *Lonely Planet*, *Refinery 29*, *Culture Trip*, *Morocco World News*, *Coldnoon*, *Past-Ten*, and *Wry Times*

"*I Probably Should've Brought a Tent* is eloquent, witty, funny, and serious all at the same time. Shonstrom's book is filled with captivating wilderness stories. He places you directly beside him in his stories and you feel the highs and lows of what he experienced. These stories quickly pull you into his journeys, flying through the pages, and yearning for more at the end! You won't be disappointed picking this one up off the shelf."

—Scott Wurdinger, author of *Philosophical Issues in Adventure Education* and *Teaching for Experiential Learning*

I Probably Should've Brought a Tent

Misadventures of a Wilderness Instructor

Erik Shonstrom

Guilford, Connecticut

An imprint of Globe Pequot, the trade division of
The Rowman & Littlefield Publishing Group, Inc.
4501 Forbes Blvd., Ste. 200
Lanham, MD 20706
www.rowman.com

Distributed by NATIONAL BOOK NETWORK

British Library Cataloguing in Publication Information available

Library of Congress Cataloging-in-Publication Data
Names: Shonstrom, Erik, author.
Title: I probably should've brought a tent : misadventures of a wilderness instructor / Erik
    Shonstrom.
Other titles: I probably should have brought a tent
Description: Guilford, Connecticut : Lyons Press, [2022] | Includes index.
Identifiers: LCCN 2021061006 (print) | LCCN 2021061007 (ebook) | ISBN 9781493060566
    (Paperback : acid-free paper) | ISBN 9781493060573 (ePub)
Subjects: LCSH: Shonstrom, Erik—Humor. | Outdoor recreation—Humor. | Outdoor life—
    Humor. | Survival—Humor. | Outward bound schools—Humor.
Classification: LCC GV191.6 .S53 2022 (print) | LCC GV191.6 (ebook) | DDC
    796.502/07—dc23/eng/20220125
LC record available at https://lccn.loc.gov/2021061006
LC ebook record available at https://lccn.loc.gov/2021061007

♾️™ The paper used in this publication meets the minimum requirements of American National
Standard for Information Sciences—Permanence of Paper for Printed Library Materials, ANSI/
NISO Z39.48-1992.

For Cynthia, love of my life, ballast and bearing

And in loving memory of Marion Winifred Crider Shonstrom
1941–1992

I love you more than you love me
Oh no you could not possibly

CONTENTS

Author's Note

YEARS AGO I WAS A REPORTER FOR A SMALL-TOWN VERMONT NEWSPAper. I covered the municipal beat—city council, schools, police. I wrote frequently about stormwater projects. I nearly fell asleep writing these articles; reading them must have been lethal.

I remember sitting in the editorial office while Donna, our acerbic managing editor, formatted a piece I'd just filed.

"Were there actually twenty?" she asked.

"What?"

Donna—who, in addition to editing the paper, was the treasurer of the regional Little League division, where she no doubt inspired the same fear in dues-paying parents as she did in greenhorn reporters—spoke without taking her eyes from the screen where she adjusted columns and cut and pasted text.

"Your article says there were twenty people at the Development Review Board meeting. Were there?"

"I think so," I said. I felt a trap being laid.

"Did you count them?"

I had not. Twenty was a guess, and I told her so.

She swiveled in her chair to face me. On a good day she was maybe five foot three. Brown hair, olive skin. No-nonsense fleece vest and leggings with clogs. Everything neat as a pin. Her eyes locked on mine. I'll never forget her next words: "This is journalism. Don't write 'twenty' unless you count."

She then turned back to her screen to continue laying out the next day's issue. When the paper came out, I paged through until I found my piece on the meeting.

There was no mention of how many people had attended.

The lesson stuck with me. If something is called journalism—or nonfiction, for that matter—it should be true. Not just kind of true, or more or less true, but as true as possible. I realize memory is faulty. I know we embellish certain episodes of our past, gloss over others, conveniently order events to fit narratives. But I believe—as cranky and old fashioned as it may be—that if you say a thing is true, it should be. Every effort should be made to be faithful to what happened.

I'm out of step with others on this, I know. Geoff Dyer, the brilliant English writer, is known to blur the lines between fiction and nonfiction. Essayist John D'Agata—notorious for his artistic interpretation of the truth—and his fact checker, Jim Fingal, argued so vehemently about what constitutes fact that the editorial process (usually hidden behind drafts and inboxes) got published as a book called *The Lifespan of a Fact*. When I found out the opening paragraph of Annie Dillard's *A Pilgrim at Tinker's Creek*—where a tomcat returning from its nocturnal prowls leaves bloody paw prints on Dillard's blankets—was not Dillard's story at all, but an anecdote she lifted from a student (with permission), I was crushed. I love that opening paragraph. To find out it wasn't exactly true; well, it took some of the raw joy out of it. For me.

The aforementioned folks are brilliant and I'm a huge fan of their work. Their derring-do stylistically is something I can only marvel at. My quiver contains a slightly less sexy arrow. I try to be accurate. To tell the truth. No matter how shame-inducing or cringey.

Everything in these pages happened. Various bits have been read and verified by individuals in the actual stories. Names have been changed out of respect for privacy. Any omissions, misrepresentations, or mistakes are completely my own. I really did fall into a latrine once.

No one is clamoring for another book by some white dude about the transcendence possible in nature. I mean, *come on*. Gag me with a Nalgene. But we all have a story, and this one is mine to tell. I hope I've done it justice.

1

The Wild Never Was

I have had to come so far away from it in order to understand it all.
—Lawrence Durrell

I'm not sure what I feared more: the sheer fifty-foot drop behind me or another minute without coffee.

For reasons lost to time and memory, I had chosen this particular week to try to kick my coffee habit. Perhaps I'd gotten it in my head that my addiction to the bitter bean was out of control, and thought that I should curtail my caffeine intake. After all, I was living in Los Angeles at the time, surrounded by people who saw self-betterment as an extreme sport, and maybe I thought if I gave up my vices I might be able to improve my figure, clear my head, and land a $20 million contract with MGM Studios. Why, in my youthful idealism, I figured the best week to go cold turkey was when taking a group of thirty middle schoolers rock climbing in Joshua Tree is beyond me. What I do know is that in terms of stupid things I've done in my life, it ranks right up there with the time I peed on an electric fence.

I gingerly edged along the crack that was leading me where I needed to go—the apex of a huge, vaguely pyramid-shaped rock outcropping. At the very top was a wedged boulder that looked like a keystone in an archway. It would be perfect, I thought, to anchor a top rope there so the kids could try to scramble up the face. It was early morning and the sun was barely up. The kids were back at our camp ensconced in their tents. There was still a nighttime chill to the air, but I was sweating buckets from both fear and exertion, as well as caffeine withdrawal delirium tremens.

The gritty stone face I was on was rounded, so my body was being pushed ever so slightly outward. I felt exposed and unbalanced, with only a few feet to go before the wedged boulder. My harness, though jangling with cams and nuts (little metal anchors of various kinds that rock climbers wedge into cracks to secure ropes), wasn't tied to anything. I was "free climbing" without a rope, an uncaffeinated Alex Honnold copycat.

I had "back-climbed" the pyramid-shaped cliff, easily getting nearly all the way to the top up the slanted slope on the other side. But the only way to get to the spot where I wanted to anchor our ropes was along this hairline crack, into which I'd wedged my climbing shoes and was now inching along. There were no handholds on the big flat face on which my body was pressed, so my arms were outstretched and I was trying to adhere my open hands to the rock gecko style.

Breathing hard, heart hammering, I pushed my foot another little bit along the crack. Not much more to go. I had to move in tiny increments, keeping my body as flat as possible to avoid pitching backward. It had seemed at first glance that this was a relatively easy way to access the spot I needed. Now that I was somewhat stranded on this sheer wall with no handholds, however, the idea that I could do this without being roped seemed idiotic. Pausing for breath, I craned my head slightly to look back over my shoulder. The desert was lighting up with the morning sun. My head was aching from caffeine deprivation and my thoughts were muzzy, but as I looked out over the expanse of desert and at the cruel rocks four stories below me, I realized I'd put myself in a predicament where I could, very possibly, die. This was deeply depressing to me, because I knew that if I pitched backward and fell to a bloody death on the rocks below, my last thought wouldn't be of loved ones or family. I wouldn't see my life flash before my eyes, a parade of people I cared for and experienced life with. I wouldn't behold my wife's face, or imagine my daughter's hand in mine as we crossed the street. I would die with only one thought in my head: *Sure would love a coffee right about now.*

I took another baby step, stretching out my right hand toward the big rock at the top of the climb. A few more inches. Almost there. I kept my balance—barely—and was able to finally get a handhold. I threw an anchor in one of the cracks and made myself fast to the rock. My body was slack with relief, and sweat soaked my shirt. I began to shake, the aftereffects of adrenaline and fear coursing through my body. *That was close*, I thought. The next thought came with such ringing clarity I can still remember it after all these years; it was like a billboard was instantaneously constructed right in front of my eyeballs with my thoughts emblazoned in neon: *What am I doing out here?*

A fair question. I had been leading outdoor adventures since I was nineteen. I could've been a lot of things: tube sock model, professional bikini-sniffer, Vanilla Ice impersonator. But I had, by dint of desire and fate, become an outdoor educator. I made a dubious living dragging young people out into the deserts, forests, and mountains to build self-reliance, develop teamwork, and poop in holes like a troglodyte.

Especially when I was younger, I'd head out into these open places on adventures and see myself as the star of the movie of my life, the plucky protagonist we're all rooting for. What I didn't get was that my own tiny story was being enacted against a backdrop of a much larger and more vicious tale. The story of white settlers clearing the land of its Indigenous people to create an untrammeled playground for people like me. After all, as a six-foot, three-inch white guy, I looked like the poster child for Manifest Destiny.

I headed out into these places that were "unpeopled" and "wild"— vast landscapes with nothing but chaparral and rocks and lizards. I would stride about these natural vistas like some colonial baron, overseeing my domain and acting as though I owned the place. I was like the gouty early colonists who purchased the entire western half of the Mississippi River basin without even thinking about the millions of Native Americans who lived there. The modern equivalent would be selling someone a "lovely undeveloped thirteen-mile-long island at the mouth of the Hudson River." It's painful to admit, but I gradually came to realize the cruel truth: White people like me are goombahs. We're the elevator farters of history.

As hard as I tried, I couldn't stay ignorant forever. I gradually came to see that the myth of virgin, pristine wilderness was exactly that, a myth. Accounts differ, but most historians and anthropologists and number-crunching geeks agree that before Columbus arrived in 1492, there were tens of millions of Native Americans occupying every corner of the Western Hemisphere, from the frozen ice of the North Sea to the wind-whipped mountains of Patagonia. What I saw initially as a tabula rasa where I could adventure to write my own epic life story, I realized was a landscape that already held countless stories. That I was, in effect, a visitor. A tourist. I was walking through a landscape soaked with the blood of

Indigenous peoples, and my own ancestors—furriers from Minnesota and Mennonites from Pennsylvania—were the cause of their demise.

I know, I know: It sounds like sententious soapboxing. But the complication, as I saw it, was that while I acknowledged the memories of these places and the trauma that had played out there, I also loved it. The trees, mountaintops, valleys; the whole fresh air thing just clicked with me. Whether scrabbling up the rocks in Joshua Tree or wading through the swamps of Florida, I felt like myself when I was in nature, despite the creeping realization that I was a usurper.

I also knew I was woefully underequipped to deal with the real world, or a real job. I'd tried and failed spectacularly in a number of professions. I just can't seem to care about institutional priorities or the machinations of business. I agree with humorist Dave Barry who wrote, "If you had to identify, in one word, the reason why the human race has not achieved, and never will achieve, its full potential, that word would be 'meetings.'"

I knew, as I clung to that rock wall—and I know it now—that there is something in my temperament that is ill-suited for profitable, normal employment; deep-seated personality flaws I seem incapable of overcoming. I think many folks who seek respite in the outdoors do it because they just don't feel like they belong anywhere else. The boardrooms and cubicles and classrooms feel like involuntary confinement, and so they strike out in search of a place where they can be themselves.

I always sought out experiences outdoors. Even from a young age, I was driven by an urge to get outdoors and wander around. The two factors that have defined the course of my life are a love of inclement weather and poor decision-making capabilities.

The first is equally a product of circumstance and genetics. I was raised in the mountains of Vermont, where the weather is so predictably awful there's an added season to the normal rotation of spring, summer, fall, and winter to fully capture the schizophrenic meteorology of the state: "mud season." In addition, my father's side of the family is Scandinavian, my mother's Scottish, so a love of rainy, cold, depressingly cloudy landscapes is a birthright. I am told that this affection for unpleasant climes is shared by others, particularly the British, whose famously rainy weather has driven them to solutions such as Wellington boots and the colonization of India.

This propensity for grinning cheerfully into the face of a driving rain or whistling happily like a man-child as I tromp through snow in subzero temperatures is, I fully acknowledge, a major character flaw. Worse, it's a proclivity that has veered into sadomasochistic tendencies, as it makes me especially happy to inflict exposure to adverse elements on children.

The inability to make thoughtful choices has plagued me my whole life. A normal adult weighs options, considers stakeholders, then acts in accordance with common sense and an understanding of cause and effect. I, on the other hand, tend to act impulsively, making major life choices on a whim, driven more by fanciful notions than prudence. The reins of my brain have been given over to the overenthusiastic golden retriever of my worst impulses.

Case in point: I grew up in the Green Mountains in a forested valley. My parents ran a bed-and-breakfast and Nordic ski center out of a nineteenth-century farmhouse. There was still a working dairy farm on the property run by an old couple that lived nearby, George and Elise. My earliest memories are of a house full of strangers, and parents who were so frightfully busy cooking and cleaning for inn guests that I enjoyed radical liberty through benign neglect.

I'd often wander about the farm and fields, poking around for something to do or hanging out with the taciturn George, an iconic Vermonter who rarely spoke a word. My greatest joy was when "Uncle" George, as I called him, would hoist me up to ride beside him on his tractor as he headed out into the hay fields to spread manure. To a kid like me, getting to witness firsthand several hundred gallons of bovine poop flung twenty feet into the air in a great, splattering rooster tail bordered on the sublime.

One March day in particular stands out. There's a saying in Vermont: "If you don't like the weather, wait twenty minutes." The previous day had been warm, so the deep snow had begun to soften. Overnight, the temperature plummeted to single digits. The result was that the snow acquired an icy glaze on the surface: a thick, hardened veneer of glasslike ice covered the ground. An adult trying to walk on the snow would crunch through, but the frozen layer could support a child just fine. My sister and I strapped on our ice skates and skated around on top of the snow through the fields and forests, slaloming through trees and racing across meadows.

We eventually began exploring an old logging road that ascended the side of the valley. We came to a spot at the top where a steep hill dropped away at our feet. It was forested by a mixed stand of maple and pine, but there was just enough space between the trunks for a straight shot down the vertiginous pitch. We'd already discovered that the icy surface of the snow and our light bodies turned every hill, no matter how gentle the slope, into a slick slide. We didn't even need sleds; our butts worked just fine.

But this hill was of a different order. Steep and forested. A kid who slid down would be putting themselves in danger of grievous bodily harm.

"Let's go!" I yelled. But my sister—older by two years—was the ranking sibling, so she got to go first. She shoved herself off, scooching on her butt but quickly picking up speed, rocketing down the hill like some pint-sized bobsledder with a death wish. As she neared light speed, I watched her face hit a low branch and her head snap back. Even from the top of the hill, I could see the bright red blood on the snow where she spun to a stop.

This was the defining moment. A normal kid would view the destruction laid out before them, wrought by the Arctic Hill of Death, and work out in the reptilian part of their brain the basic calculus that it was dangerous. I, on the other hand, scooted forward and followed my sister, picking up speed and rocketing down on my bum as she sat bleeding and wailing below.

I crashed—spectacularly—into a more forgiving evergreen. The rest is a blur: my parents arriving to scoop up my crying, bloodied sister, a trip to the hospital, her return with stitches in her lip.

Here we have the germinal seed of my personality: a deep-seated ignorance of cause and effect. But something else as well: a love of the unpredictable, an eagerness for experience seasoned with inappropriate amounts of blithe disregard for propriety. Despite the narrow confines of my life, I've tried to get out and about and see what the world has to offer.

7

While I acknowledge it's a fault, I'm not particularly keen on analysis and contemplation (to which my children, who've consumed meals I've made that go beyond fusion and enter into the gastronomical realm of the multiverse, can attest), and would prefer, whenever possible, to just *do something* rather than talk about it. So it's hardly surprising that one of my first jobs was as an Outward Bound instructor, leading incarcerated youth on river trips in Florida. Which makes sense, as I'm temperamentally incapable of tucking in my shirt.

I'd go on to lead trips in the Sierra, Vermont, Puget Sound, even Mexico and Europe. I would take students into landscapes that weren't mine, really. I was colonizing—dressing up in organic wool pullovers and recycled-plastic puffy jackets and preaching Leave No Trace ethics, but colonizing nonetheless. I played the part of a bumbling, anodyne conquistador.

But none of this was on my mind as I secured the anchors on the top of the pyramid-shaped boulder in the middle of Joshua Tree National Park. Despite the fact that I'd almost killed myself due to a deeply flawed and quickly abandoned attempt at self-improvement, I began to feel tiny sparks of what resembled happiness. I was tired and coffee-deprived, and also entertaining growing fears about how the regularity of my bowel movements would be affected sans caffeine, but I was able to enjoy, at least a little, the beauty of the place I was in. Once I was sure I'd double-anchored the top rope, I clipped in and began to rappel down. Looking back over my shoulder, I saw the desert and the sun, the rocks and the sand, and felt, for a fleeting instant, that I was right where I should be.

2

RIFA

They are already dead ... those who had lost track of their own absurdity.

—Shirley Hazzard

The night hummed and crackled around me with life: chirps, buzzes, squawks. Moths dive-bombed my headlamp. I felt an insect chomp my ankle, then another behind my knee. In Vermont, mosquitoes and blackflies can be a nuisance, but what I quickly realized is the mosquitoes biting me in Florida were in a different league. It was like someone was dancing around me under Harry Potter's invisibility cloak with a cattle prod, zinging me with abandon. Each bite brought a sharp, stabbing, wasp-sting pain. I slapped and swore, stamping my feet. Panicking, somehow I got the tent up into a rough facsimile of shelter and dove in through the door, pushing my sleeping bag in front of me and hysterically zipping the screen shut.

But somehow all the mosquitoes had gotten in the tent with me. They continued to bite everywhere now; I felt their needle-like proboscises stabbing my ribs, back, arms, even my face. Trying to muffle my screams, I wriggled into my sleeping bag despite the oppressive, armpit-like heat and humidity of the Florida outback. The stings kept coming. Popping my head out of the stifling bag, I used my headlamp to examine my body, and that's when I saw them.

I was covered in fire ants.

I had unknowingly pitched my tent on an anthill populated by *Solenopsis invicta* Buren, commonly known as the red imported fire ant, or RIFA.

The next period of time exists in my memory as a shattered, frenetic series of jump-cuts. Me, twisting wildly about as I pinched ants off my body, their mandibles visibly jabbing my skin; a frenzied, tent-bound discotheque striptease as my headlamp strobes wildly and I twist and writhe, ripping off clothing; half-muffled screams and curses that sound as if I'm speaking in tongues.

I spent the night hunting down ants in my tent, crushing their little exoskeletons while my body buzzed with painful bites. I was too embarrassed to sprint back to the bunkhouse and admit my stupidity, yet sweatily desired nothing more than to escape the sheer hellishness of a tent infested with fire ants. Caught between a self-imposed Scylla and Charybdis of idiocy. I barely slept, as the occasional well-hidden ant wriggled out of hiding and made its location known with yet another savage bite.

I was in Scottsmoor, Florida—a godforsaken place to begin with, fire ants notwithstanding—to train as a wilderness instructor with Outward Bound. Training I clearly needed, as I aptly demonstrated that first night. The landscape around Scottsmoor doesn't look like stereotypical Florida. No glitzy schmaltz of the beach cities farther south, no soul-sucking tourist lures of Epcot and Disney. But it's still Florida, so it's flat and hot. Gridded by dusty roads, Vidalia onion fields alternate with orange groves.

Earlier in the evening, at the tender age of nineteen, I landed at the Orlando airport to begin my training as an Outward Bound instructor. I was nervous and unsure of what to expect. I had lived practically my whole life in rural Vermont, and it showed. I was untraveled, unworldly, and clueless. I'd never eaten sushi and believed 1980s movies to be the zenith of civilization. I wandered aimlessly among the massive gleaming terminals, looking for the lead trainers who were supposed to pick me up. It was late in the evening, and the hordes of tourists had already passed through on their way to The Happiest Place on Earth. The only thing that would've completed the image of the yokel out of his depths would've been if I was barefoot with straw clamped between my teeth, a burlap sack flung over my shoulder.

A man ran toward me. A shock of curly terrier hair haloed his high forehead, a giant grin showcasing his diastema. Good omen. A gap-toothed smile was indicative of puckish intelligence and mischievous goodwill—see Eddie Murphy, Madonna, Woody Harrelson, and Samuel L. Jackson.

"You must be Erik!" he said, panting. "Finally found you. I'm Pete."

Pete was one of the other trainees. I'd later learn he'd been in the army. He'd also worked in Antarctica, driving a forklift and doing odd jobs for researchers. He had the personality of a poodle, all bounce and goofy exuberance. Pete was just past thirty, but we bonded despite more than a decade separating us. We both, by circuitous routes involving shared peripatetic employment habits, had signed up to be trained as Outward Bound instructors and had arrived in Florida for a few weeks of orientation.

Outward Bound was started in England in 1941 by educator Kurt Hahn, a German Jew who spoke out against Hitler during the 1930s, got imprisoned, then fled to England where he zealously threw himself into education and created a number of different schools. The inception of Outward Bound—an organization taking students on rigorous outdoor adventures with the aim of building confidence and teamwork skills—resulted from Hahn noticing that older sailors fared better than young whippersnappers when faced with dire survival circumstances. Hahn saw the need for a school that taught outdoor skills, but also attempted to engender the kind of patient resilience he saw as essential to coping with extreme outdoor challenges. "To serve, to strive, and not to yield," became the Outward Bound motto. Now, outdoor programs and wilderness schools have proliferated across the world, with giants like the National Outdoor Leadership School (NOLS) sharing a piece of the Outward Bound pie. But Hahn created one of the first of its kind. If various historical records are to be taken at face value, Hahn was a complicated individual; his accomplishments were numerous but contrasted sharply with other personality attributes, including a propensity for discipline involving a stout cane and an overbearing personality. You can take the man out of Germany, but you can't take Germany out of the man, I guess.

Instructor orientation was a few weeks long, during which we'd learn to paddle canoes on the rivers and lakes of Florida in preparation to become Outward Bound instructors in its Youth at Risk program. Incarcerated kids would join us for thirty-day river trips once we were all trained up.

I helped Pete gather up a few other straggling trainees and we all jumped in a van driven by Jon, one of the lead instructors, and headed to basecamp in Scottsmoor.

It was dark by the time we got to camp. There were maybe a dozen other trainees, all in their twenties. I was the youngest, Pete the oldest.

The Scottsmoor basecamp was just a simple double-wide ranch house with a bunkhouse behind it, surrounded by palmettos and scrubby copses giving way to agricultural fields.

Like most teenagers, I was susceptible to a soul-crushing amount of insecurity for which I overcompensated with false bravado and embarrassingly obvious posturing. I keenly felt my age and lack of experience after spending a few minutes with the other trainees—most had graduated college—and noted a deficit in both outdoor and more elementary life skills: no bank account, stumped by the logic of filing taxes, understood female anatomy about as clearly as quantum theory. Thus, I was eager to overcompensate and prove that I was a capable outdoorsperson, ready to face whatever challenges the outback of Florida could offer. It was late, and as bunks were chosen, I volunteered to pitch a tent out in the yard. Jon and Heather, the instructors who'd be training us, looked puzzled but shrugged. I grabbed one of the tents we'd be using during the course and blundered out into the yard.

It was dark. I had a cheap headlamp that I strapped on and began trying to assemble the tent. After a few frustrated attempts I finally began to make headway, threading recalcitrant aluminum poles through little nylon sleeves. It was at that point I began to make the acquaintance of the RIFA ants and endured a long, sleepless, miserable night.

As soon as the sun streaked the sky I left the tent, taking care to step over the now-obvious anthill right on my doorstep, covered in my sneaker prints. I quietly made my way to the bathroom, and stared in horror at my shirtless reflection in the mirror.

It looked like I'd been slammed by atomic-force puberty. Fire ant bites turn into little pus-filled whiteheads. I was covered in what looked like zits. Hideously disfigured, I waited in a shame spiral until I heard others waking and shuffling over to the kitchen. Mortified, I made my appearance.

I was teased and given some advice. Don't pop the stings; it risks infection. Avoid ant hills (duh). As I awkwardly stood with everyone else drinking bad coffee, the stories began. My own humiliation had acted as a prompt, and stories of stings, bites, and poor decisions began to flow. I gradually began to feel a bit less like an idiot. As Kyle, a bearded Georgian, related a story about a wasp nest in an old car, I murmured to Pete that it was nice to hear others had made mistakes like mine.

"I don't know," he said. "Yours was pretty dumb."

If there is some grand creator out there conjuring worlds, then surely Florida is their attempt at a joke. Equatorially hot, it contains staggeringly beautiful natural areas: the Everglades, the Crystal River, white sand beaches, the Keys. Yet it's also the tackiest place on earth. Disney, wizard theme parks, SeaWorld, and Universal Studios conjure images of hungover parents, red-faced and sweaty, herding their offspring through endless lines of bloated vacationers all eager to throw away a year of savings on reckless purchases of inflatable rodents and overpriced gastrointestinally dangerous food. One imagines them home after a week or so in Mickey and Minnie country, surrounded by suitcases exploded with dirty tank tops and grimy flip-flops, collapsed in a heap on the couch staring vacantly at the wall, murmuring, "Wha . . . what happened?"

There are creatures crawling around the swamps and backcountry of Florida that are Jurassic in stature and temperament. Invasive Burmese pythons have made a home for themselves—and they're from an Asian jungle. But they're perfectly content to hang in Florida, as it checks all the python boxes. Hot? Yep. Wet? Yep. Filled with lots of things to eat? Yep. How do Floridians respond? By creating a therapeutic support group for former soldiers with PTSD. The vets hunt down and kill Burmese pythons in an attempt to work through the violence of warfare. *That could only happen in Florida.* In fact, if the internet is to be believed, one of the pythons actually tried to eat an alligator. When a snake is so carelessly predatory it tries to eat another large reptile that's a cross between a Buick and Godzilla, you know it means business.

The history of Florida is a chaotic one. Syphilis-ridden conquistadors and slavers landed there throughout the 1500s, usually on a stereotypical trip of plunder, resource theft, enslavement, and Indigenous genocide. The usual colonial menu. Juan Ponce de León is often credited with being the first white person to land in Florida, though this is disputed. He had a notorious career in the Caribbean and South Atlantic, joining Christopher Columbus on his second voyage, running slaving businesses on Puerto Rico and elsewhere. In fact, it's estimated that a significant percentage of people in Puerto Rico can trace their ancestry to Ponce de León, which must be like having the last name "Manson" or "Kaczynski" on your Tinder profile. It bears noting that Ponce de León wasn't merely an accessory to the violence of early colonialism in the Caribbean; he was a murderous military commander. In Hispaniola (modern-day Haiti and Dominican Republic) he put down an uprising known as the Higuey massacre in which members of the Taíno people—men, women, and children—were disemboweled and had their hands and feet hacked off by the Spanish. He traveled to Florida twice, and like many Spanish was seeking slaves and basically whatever he could grab. Inexplicably, there are statues of Juan Ponce de León to this day in both Puerto Rico and Ponte Vedra Beach in Florida, which is sort of like having a monument to the world's biggest hemorrhoid.

But, Florida being Florida, it's the locale for at least one exception to the rule of violent European colonial dispossession of native culture and lives. It's home to the Seminole people, the only tribe that never officially surrendered in the face of the US pogroms of the nineteenth century that attempted to wipe out native populations. Eventually, the US military just gave up hunting down the Indigenous peoples of Florida, who'd taken refuge in the impenetrable swamps. If there is a geographical equivalent to giving the middle finger, it's Florida.

But during my brief time there I'd come to love it. It was a love like the mom has for her homicidal son in that movie *We Need to Talk About Kevin*. I know Florida is dangerous, filled with both creatures and people out of nightmares. But for the most part, I still feel tenderly toward her. Exploring the rivers and lakes of Florida changed the way I saw the state. I got to spend weeks at a time drifting on slow currents of water the color of weak tea that snaked through dense palm and hardwood forests. Paddling quietly, I'd watch pterodactyl-like herons flapping overhead. Cottonmouth snakes would be sunning themselves on half-submerged logs. Once, paddling in ocean waters just off the coast, I saw a small shark dart from the shadows and watched it glide underneath me through the water. Late at night, camped on the shores of brackish lakes, I'd shine my headlamp out over the water and see the dull red eyes of alligators looking back.

While much of the state was chockablock strip malls and concrete, getting outside and on the rivers gave a glimpse of just how rugged, jungly, and wild Florida could be. But it wasn't just the place; what I was doing—working with kids outdoors—was something I loved. I threw myself into it wholeheartedly.

A fair question to ask would be: Why? What's the point of outdoor education? After all, most of us end up flipping burgers or answering emails or selling Mitsubishis for a living. The ability to safely ford a river or construct a shelter out of leaves and logs hardly seems necessary. For example, despite my deep-seated antipathy for long department meetings, I've never had to rig an emergency rappel rope to escape out the window (yet).

If it's not about hard skills like building a snow cave or orienteering in the bush, then it's about what it shifts for us internally. How it changes—sometimes subtly, sometimes dramatically—the very landscape of our souls. This isn't to say that everyone who takes an Outward Bound or NOLS course experiences a transcendental moment as they traverse scree-covered ridges at 12,000 feet with a forty-pound pack wobbling on their back. But moments like that broaden our perspective of who we are. Rigorous outdoor adventures *deepen* who we are. I'm not sure you can say the same thing about learning to calculate compound interest or how to code in C++.

3

Breakfast with Lars

SOMEONE WAS HAMMERING ON MY DOOR IN THE STEAMY PREDAWN. I lurched to wakefulness, heart thumping. Groping my way to the door in darkness, I yanked it open. There stood Lars, in a tiny pair of running shorts, hair neatly tied back in a braid.

"Yah, we are running now!?"

My cabin at the Yulee basecamp was approximately the size of a SpongeBob suitcase a child would take for the weekend to Disneyland. The close confines meant that a healthy fart could suffocate in mere seconds—a scenario I'd tested nightly after consuming what passed for dinner at basecamp.

I mumbled some sort of acknowledgment and began hunting around for my shorts and socks. The not-quite-morning air hummed with insect life. The sky had the slightest of glows to the east, either the rising sun or the Stuckey's truck stop a mile or so away. The sun was still below the horizon—not that I could see the horizon through the dense scrub forest around us.

Lars resembled a pint-sized Arnold Schwarzenegger in physique and bearing. He had harsh, Teutonic good looks. You could imagine him beating someone up for information in a Stasi interrogation room with a smile. He was Scandinavian—Swedish, I believe—and how he ended up working with us among teenage felons in Florida, I never knew or have long since forgotten.

He took off like a deer. Lars didn't run so much as prance up on the balls of his feet. There was a gliding buoyancy to his stride, as though gravity had less of a claim on him than the rest of us. The perfect inverted triangle of his trapezius muscles led me into the thick undergrowth down a narrow trail. How does someone even *get* muscles on their back like that?

People experience their first moments of wakefulness differently. My wife, for example, is on a very different wavelength than I am upon rising from the waters of sleep. As we begin to shift and stretch, eyes barely open in the early morning, she'll turn to me—and it's like walking into an auctioneer's pitch midstream: "Finn has violin today but we also need to pick up the prescription before swimming I'm really worried that if we don't transfer money out of saving over to checking the account is going to be at zero if that appliance guy doesn't call back I swear to God can you call the school and make sure they know Finn won't be there Friday when's the last time you even called your dad . . ."

My own internal monologue is more along the lines of "Mph. Coffee, whatz . . . coffee."

It appeared Lars woke with all cylinders firing. I tried to keep up as best I could. I am not the fastest guy out there. I don't have spring-like tension in my tendons and muscles. I'm built rather loosely, like an Ikea desk after it's been around for a few years and moved three times: Screws are stripped, pressboard is flaking, one side is propped up with a wad of paper because it's uneven. Wobbly but functional. I could practically hear the vitality surging through Lars's veins.

He zipped down the trail, the distance between us growing by the second. Immediately I began to fabricate excuses for why I was slow should he stop to wait for me: twisted ankle, recovering from a shark bite, just donated a kidney, hypoglycemic. Through the greasy sheen of sweat already stinging my eyes I saw Lars bob, low, like a boxer, then spring back to the center of the trail without breaking his gazelle-like stride. I had only a moment to wonder why he'd performed this little maneuver before it happened. I ran straight into the massive web of a spider. Strands pasted themselves across my face. I felt filaments of silk bind my arms and legs, surprisingly springy and resilient. I frantically brushed a hand across my face and chest. As I did, my hand hit what felt like a crab clinging to my shirt.

Golden orb weavers (which Floridians have given the innocuous and misleadingly cute nickname of "banana spider") can be huge, with a leg span the size of a child's hand. I don't know if the one I ran into was that big, because I was busy having a nervous breakdown and vividly remembering the scene from *Alien* where the extraterrestrial latches onto John Hurt's face and lays eggs down his throat. I let loose a little scream—okay, probably a large, soul-rending shriek—and began to wildly swat the web and spider as I careened down the narrow trail hacked through the Florida outback. Lars didn't slow his pace. He called back cheerfully over his shoulder, "Yah, those spiders are *everywhere!*"

Lars kept running, and I tried to keep up, but his little Scandinavian form receded in the distance. I couldn't keep pace. My ambitions for physical exercise have always outstripped my follow-through. During most of my life, I've been one of those people who go out for the evening, drink a half dozen beers, gorge on pizza and fries, stumble home, and eat bowls of cereal while mainlining *Game of Thrones* before falling into bed. I'd wake up bloated and bilious, head thudding, eyes red. I'd bumble to the bathroom and catch a glimpse of myself in the sink mirror. Swollen, sagging flesh. Skin the greasy sheen of sausage that's just gone off. "No more!" I'd resolutely say to my reflection. "From here on out, a new leaf!" I'd throw on some running shorts and a T-shirt and go for a shambling, dry-heaving run over spectacular distances like some medieval penitent fixed on absolution. I'd do burpees and lift weights and run hill sprints, my red stop sign face looking like the business end of a baboon. Joints loose, head clanging. "A new life starts now," I'd tell myself. After my masochistic workout I'd go through my day, overly pleased at the soul-cleansing I'd provided for myself. I'd returned from the self-flagellating depths of hell, persevered through the gassy repercussions of a night out in Sodom and Gomorrah. Triumphant, I'd celebrate with a beer, and start all over again.

I pawed at the webs coating my face and danced away, cringing and cutting the early morning air with colorful phrases. Lars had disappeared, outdistancing me in minutes. I shuffled along, filled with revulsion and shame. Nothing could make the morning any worse, I believed.

Finally, after getting lost on the winding trails surrounding basecamp, I found my way back. Looking forward to coffee and breakfast and a shower, I walked toward the main part of camp where the large outdoor showers were located. Enclosed within a scrappy wooden fence, we had a few rusty showerheads that sporadically sprinkled out room temperature water. I opened the gate and stumbled in.

"Yah, you finally made it!"

Lars was already well sudsed and brimming with hygienic enthusiasm. His nakedness was aesthetically perfect. The pube to genital ratio was, I believe, mathematically congruent to the golden mean. His body was flawless, like it was designed in a cryogenic lab.

I grunted back at him and peeled off my running clothes. By contrast, my naked body looked like a boiled chicken, all knobby limbs and angles. My butt looked like fourteen pounds of cold mashed potatoes. I ducked under the sprinkle of the showerhead farthest from Lars, who was now vigorously scrubbing his body with a loofa sponge. I hadn't even brought soap, and so just stood there trying not to look at Lars, who was now singing Bon Jovi in his thick accent. "Yah! You're halfway there! Yah! Living on a prayer!" I wondered briefly what the homicide laws were in that part of Florida.

After our shower we headed into the communal kitchen for breakfast. Lars was very methodical about breakfast, making sure he had equal parts protein, fiber, fruit, and vitamins. He always brought what looked like toothpaste tubes filled with salmon and herring pastes and would smear it on toast, which I felt broke some inviolable culinary law prohibiting fish at breakfast and should be prosecuted to the fullest extent.

As the other instructors began arriving, Lars greeted each with a hale and hearty welcome and began regaling the room with scenes from our morning run. "Yah, and you should have heard him scream!" he yodeled to the amusement of everyone there. I smiled weakly, stuffing my face with coffee and toast, wishing I'd gotten a job in some mail room where I could sort envelopes in a dark basement and be left mercifully alone.

We headed out into the early morning Florida sunshine. Lars came bounding up behind me, clapping me on the shoulder.

"We run again tomorrow, yah Erik?"

"Sure," I mumbled, smiling weakly.

4

Jacked by Dolphins

To be a Negro in this country and to be relatively conscious is to be in a rage almost all the time.

—James Baldwin

Derek Mason was a scrappy fifteen-year-old Black kid who'd been locked up in the Jacksonville version of little-kid prison for armed robbery. He wasn't big—barely came to my shoulder—but was built like a loaded spring. He had the body of a flyweight boxer. His waist was trim, and his arms and torso had the sort of sinewy strength and grace that dancers have. Or adolescents who spend six months in a juvenile penitentiary fighting for their life.

Derek got dropped off two days early for a thirty-day canoe trip due to the wonders of bureaucracy emanating from some dingy office of the Department of Youth and Families in Jacksonville. Having finished orientation training and been baptized by the RIFA ants, I had been assigned a role as an assistant instructor for Outward Bound's Youth At Risk program. I ended up stationed at the Yulee basecamp. Yulee is located in the very northeastern corner of Florida, a densely wooded, scrubby area filled with armadillos and snakes. All of a sudden, we had a kid at basecamp a few days early, and someone had to look after him. I got babysitting detail.

I never considered my privilege during the time I spent with Outward Bound. It never occurred to me that I was this looming, goofy white guy running river trips for kids who were predominantly African American. On my first trip the lead instructor, Emmett, was Black, which I think made for a smoother experience since he could relate to the kids in a way I couldn't. On some level there was probably some white savior stuff going on. Here I was, in the Deep South, dragging young kids of color into the wilderness to teach them how to be accomplished humans. In retrospect, this had a neocolonial kind of feel—I would subdue their unacceptable tendencies. Totally ignorant of the systemic racism they'd experienced their whole lives, I approached the experience at face value. While not overtly evil, it was an ignorant way in which to engage with the kids we worked with. What I could have done was just *see* them. Be present for them. But I grew up in Vermont in the 1980s, where salt was considered a spice and you'd have to board an airplane to find soul food or a decent taco. There were very few people of color. My understanding of racial dynamics was right up there with my ability to repair O rings on the space shuttle: nonexistent.

I spent some time showing Derek around the camp. He said very little, just a nod now and then. It wasn't much of a tour and was over in less than ten minutes. We sat on the steps leading up to the main building, digging our feet nervously into the dirt and slapping at bugs. Neither of us knew what to say, I think. Derek's expression was inscrutable. Minutes ticked by, and I began to realize we'd need to figure out *something* to do.

I decided to try to make the most of the time and teach Derek to paddle a canoe. There was an estuary near the camp, and I figured we could haul a canoe to the water and paddle around. Get to know each other, build rapport and trust, and have a Hallmark After-School Special kind of moment. Some kumbaya magic.

I was a white guy asking a Black kid to get in a boat against his will. My ignorance of the traumatic, historical echo of the moment may rank up there with the dumbest things I've ever done. Upon suggesting we paddle out for a bit, Derek looked at me with what can only be described as intense skepticism. He stared hard at me, maybe trying to gauge my true intentions. Finally, he shrugged.

I convinced Derek to help me carry the canoe down to the water. The area surrounding Outward Bound's Yulee basecamp was a mix of palm scrub, deciduous trees, and large biting insects. The nearby estuary was not sugar-sand-beach Florida, trim and anodyne. It was reedy, marshy, tea-colored-water Florida. It wasn't the sort of coastline defined by artfully landscaped palms and sunburned New Jerseyites. It was tidal mudflats and saw grass. It was a decent setting for a pretty legitimate outdoor experience.

Spending time in the backwoods of Florida gave me an appreciation for all the stuff you hear about Florida: the bugs and heat and general uniqueness of the place. For the sheer weirdness of Florida, its mythology and history.

Derek and I gathered the paddles and life jackets for our expedition. To break the silence, I began chatting to him about the area and about the history of Florida. I was, at the time, particularly interested in Europeans who assimilated into Native American cultures. I had read *The Leatherstocking Tales* by James Fenimore Cooper as a kid, and *The Last of the Mohicans* starring Daniel Day Lewis had been released the year before this trip. I realize now, in retrospect, that my impromptu lecture was an early symptom of what I call "Old Man Talks about WWII" disease, a chronic condition that affects men in their later years. The illness is evidenced by a propensity for long, rambling, pointless diatribes about history that no one wants to hear. As we pulled the canoe off the rack and began lugging it down the narrow forest trail toward the water, I told Derek some of the stories I knew of early Florida history, such as that of Juan Ortiz.

Juan Ortiz was a sailor on a Spanish expedition to Florida led by Pánfilo de Narváez in 1528. Ortiz and a few others were captured by the Tocobaga tribe near modern-day Tampa Bay. The plan was to burn Ortiz alive, which, given the destruction and genocide visited upon Native Americans by waves of Europeans over four hundred years, while unlucky for Ortiz, seems a fitting response to white colonial ambitions. Chief Uzita was moving ahead with the flambé de Spaniard when his daughter, according to legend, begged him to stop and spare Ortiz.

Herein lies the slippery slope of history. Did she really? I mean, I can imagine anyone watching a human burned alive might have second thoughts and request the event be adjourned. Or is this yet another tale told to reinforce pity for the struggles of white Europeans? What we do know is that a future European colonial from the 1600s, John Smith, may have pilfered the narrative of a white man saved by an empathetic Native American daughter. In his case, the young woman was named Pocahontas. Then, some four hundred years later, Mel Gibson, a racist, anti-Semitic Australian, would provide the voice of Smith in the Disney animated version of *Pocahontas*, which does have a weird symmetry, if you think about it.

The story goes on with Ortiz living for eleven years with the Tocobaga and Mocoso peoples, learning their languages and customs. Eventually,

Hernando de Soto, another conquistador with buckets of blood on his hands, "found" Ortiz and "rescued" him.

I have a theory about this, based on a loose understanding of life for the average sixteenth-century European. Life for someone like Ortiz couldn't have been all that great prior to his decade with the Native Americans of Florida. Spain, like all of Europe, suffered from periodic bouts of plague, starvation, despotism, and poor hygiene. The sheer lack of physical comforts was appalling. For example, accounts of the sea voyages from Europe to the Americas paint an ugly picture of what daily experiences were for sailors on these transatlantic voyages.

The son of Christopher Columbus, who traveled with him on one of these colonial conquest trips to the "new world," was appalled by what he experienced onboard. "What with the dampness, our ship biscuit had become so wormy that, God help me, I saw many who waited for darkness to eat porridge made of it, that they might not see the maggots," he wrote.

Columbus's offspring was referring to hardtack biscuits, a staple of European oceanic travel, where hockey pucks of flour are baked and broken and baked again until their density is rivaled only by their lack of appeal. These orbs of digestive assault were created by the same misguided egoists who believed in Manifest Destiny, I might add. There were so many maggots in the food on these voyages, noted the adolescent Columbus, they actually comprised the main component of the food, "and others were so used to eating them that they didn't even trouble to pick them out because they might lose their supper had they been so fastidious."

So Ortiz left Spain—home of the Inquisition, where supposed "heretics" were thrown onto the rack to be stretched to death, made to drink gallons of water until their insides split, or covered in burning hot coals to extract confessions—and traveled on one of these ghastly ships with lice-infested sailors eating maggoty hardtack and trying to avoid sodomy at the hands of horny deckhands, and ended up as a prisoner of the native peoples of Florida. While we don't know everything about how the Indigenous peoples such as the Timucua or Seminole lived, we know from human remains that they were actually pretty well-fed and healthy. In fact, Columbus himself observed that native islanders seemed healthy and not nutritionally deficient, as his own crew was. In his journals he noted that the Indigenous peoples of the Caribbean had "good stature, a very handsome people" and that "their legs are very straight, all in one line, and no belly, but very well formed." No doubt a pleasant contrast to his own malnourished, syphilitic crew of mealy sailors.

My guess is that Ortiz had a better chance at a well-fed, harmonious life with the Tocobaga than he would have had in Spain. Most Indigenous peoples had relatively egalitarian societies and fair amounts of personal liberty and freedom. Their lives weren't perfect—there was internecine conflict between tribes, food shortages, all the challenges of the natural world, interpersonal disputes—but to be sure there was no crushing hierarchy or brutal religious persecution. There would have been opportunities to integrate into the rhythms and social fabric of the people. To live with a bit of ease and maybe dignity. This would have been in stark contrast to the strictures and oppressions of life for a sailor such as Ortiz. Perhaps he didn't want to be rescued at all—at least, that's how I imagine it.

I stopped talking for a bit and peeked over my shoulder at Derek. He was gamely carrying the stern of the canoe, facing downward with an expression of mute resignation. He looked smaller than I'd initially supposed him to be, dwarfed a bit by the bulky canoe and towering scrub palms surrounding us. Clearly, I was boring.

I began asking him some questions about himself, which he replied to with short, quiet answers. Derek Mason had never been out of Jacksonville. In fact, he had never really left his neighborhood. He'd never been camping, or hiking, or to a zoo. He'd never been on a boat. He could swim, but the only swimming he'd ever done was at a community pool. He'd never swum in the ocean. His experiences were anathema to my own privileged, New England upbringing. I was pathologically naïve, and never for a second tempered my nineteen-year-old bravado and considered he might be so completely out of his element that he was terrified.

At first, it was rough talking to Derek. And at second. And third. It was not easy. We didn't have common ground. He had life experiences the likes of which I couldn't imagine, but was still very childlike in many ways. It was challenging to deal with that contradiction; I didn't have the skills. I talked a lot about a whole lot of nothing. I'm pretty sure he thought I was an idiot.

I situated Derek in the bow of the canoe and pushed us off into the estuary. Derek clung gamely to his beat-up paddle. I paddled us out into the main channel, headed toward the open water of the ocean. We cruised through the saw grass as the sun blazed off the brown water. It was summer in Florida, which means a kind of soupy, hazy heat reminiscent of breathing through wet wool while sadistic beauticians blast you with hair dryers.

Derek wasn't really paddling. He was rigid in his seat, silly life vest up around his ears, his eyes frantically searching the water. He was scared, and deeply out of his element. I chatted about J-strokes and paddle techniques and other asinine subjects.

The fear was so intense Derek wouldn't heft up the gallon water jug I'd given him to drink. He was too afraid the movement would make us tip. I could see his face, when he would whip his head from left to right, scanning the water for danger, and the rictus of fear galvanized his expression into a mask of pure terror.

It was at that moment the water around us started roiling and splashing and bubbling. It was as though some huge, multi-appendaged beast was beating the water from underneath. Derek screamed a number of colorful phrases, as the splashing and frothing reached a Class V whitewater-like intensity. The splashing had started off our bow, but had quickly surrounded the boat. We were under attack.

Then we saw the dorsal fins headed toward us.

Our little fifteen-foot canoe was floating in the middle of a hundred-yard-wide estuary that led to the ocean. The banks were exposed, intertidal flats of mud and tall, bladed grasses. In the distance, the Atlantic Ocean, opening up about a half mile distant of our bow, glimmered and flashed. I could see that there was a bit of wind out there. There was no civilization nearby that we could see.

At first I thought they were sharks. A natural assumption, considering I was raised on *Jaws* movies (*Jaws III* an underrated masterpiece, in my opinion). I assumed, like most children of the 1970s and '80s, that every time I ventured into the ocean, huge great whites were cruising lazily underneath, revving up before launching upward to snap me in half.

The dorsal fins approaching me and a rapidly cursing and wide-eyed Derek did not, however, belong to sharks. They belonged to the *Delphinus* genus, otherwise known as dolphins.

One of the ways dolphins capture their prey is by herding fish toward shore, usually the muddy bank of an intertidal flat, and "washing" the fish up onto the bank. The dolphins then intentionally beach themselves as their prey flops on the bank and snatch up their lunch before flipping back into the water. The dolphins work in concert, much like border collies herding sheep.

The flopping, splashing frenzy around our boat was a school of mullet trying to escape from the dolphins. Derek and I were caught in the middle of a BBC nature program. We watched as the mullet-laden wave the dolphins pushed in front of them washed onto the shore, the luckless fish, white bellies flashing, strewn on the muddy bank. The dolphins lunged powerfully out of the water maybe fifty yards to our right. Dolphins, by the way, are BIG. Really big. There were three of them, and their battleship gray bodies looked like pure, rubber-coated muscle. Which they were.

Derek lost it. Completely, totally, and utterly lost it. It was all too much for him, understandably, and to his credit he kept a stiff upper lip for quite some time. But lunging cetaceans and rampaging mullet were just too intense. Derek was in touch with just enough sanity to realize that the boat was the only place to be safe. And that he was sharing that boat with the crazy white man responsible for putting him in this alien, terrifying, and unreal predicament.

Derek picked up his full gallon jug of water and whirled around to face me. His face was screwed up in rage, fear, and bitterness. He hurled the water jug at me.

Scientific point of reference: A full gallon of water weighs 8.35 pounds. When hurled with force, at point-blank range, it hurts like hell.

The jug hit me in the chest. Hard. The blow landed squarely, knocking me backward off my seat. The canoe rocked dangerously as I fell back, grasping at the gunwales to steady myself. Derek screamed as the boat pitched and rolled.

I picked myself up and tried to consider our options. A tipsy boat in a dolphin- and mullet-filled estuary was no place for a confrontation. I began to paddle us back toward the little creek inlet that we'd paddled down earlier. An awkward silence, heavy as the salty, humid air, descended.

Earlier, I noticed paddling seemed kind of easy. As we paddled our way toward the place we'd put in, I realized the tide had been going out—had gone out. Our little creek was gone, replaced by about three hundred feet of sulphurous, bubbling mud, crawling with crabs.

I explained to Derek that we were going to have to get out, into the thigh-deep mud, and haul the canoe back to shore over the exposed tidal flat. My suggestion was met with a stony stare that would put Mount Rushmore to shame. He was beyond annoyed, and in no mood to help. I ended up hauling him, and the canoe, through the mud. Derek sat in the canoe, clutching the sides in a death grip, his long-abandoned paddle at his feet.

We got to shore and I pulled the canoe up onto solid ground. Derek quickly jumped out of the boat. I bent to grab my water jug. Derek picked up his paddle, and as I stood, he swung. The paddle blade smacked my skull in a sharp blow.

I was knocked forward and sprawled against the canoe. I saw stars, which I had always thought was a trope reserved for Looney Toons. I raised my head woozily to see Derek's back as he walked away up the path back to camp.

Technically I should've filled out an incident report, had some kind of mediation with Derek before we headed out into the wilds of Florida for the next thirty days together. What I did was nothing. I followed Derek back to camp, gingerly touching the welt on the back of my head.

Derek was sitting near the platform tents, on the edge of the sandy parking lot, and he looked plenty pissed. But, with his arms crossed over his knees and curled up like a defiant kid, he also looked young and vulnerable. I touched the squishy bump on the back of my head. *Maybe not completely vulnerable*, I thought.

There was an odd moment when he stared at me with a mixture of hate and confusion and hurt, where we shared an unspoken understanding. We were stuck together for the next month, and we'd have to figure it out. It was that simple. And that reality was probably terrifying for him; he would be with me for a month. After an awkward silence, he followed me back down the path to the scene of my near-beheading. We picked up the canoe and lugged it back to camp.

Soon the rest of the kids arrived, piling out of white vans. A whole bunch of new kids, including a twelve-year-old named Nick called "Nick and his little man" by the other kids because he had a vaguely anthropomorphically shaped scar on his forehead where his mother had burned him with a clothes iron in a fit of rage. And Damien, a seventeen-year-old who would labor over letters to his mother that absolutely seeped with thoughtfulness. Other instructors helped mitigate my otherworldly ineptitude.

We headed out on the river and spent a few weeks exploring the backwoods of Florida together. We had our share of adventures—including a lightning strike that was so close I smelled the ozone. We played and swam in the river, growing more comfortable around each other day by day. I listened to their stories and jokes, tried to mediate arguments. I remember one stifling day we waded into the river and played keep-away with a tennis ball for hours. Laughing and splashing, I was struck by a mundane yet profound realization as we charged and blocked, ran and threw Hail Mary passes: *These kids are fun.* The day the kids left, the juvenile corrections vans showed up and waited as the kids shuffled around and gathered to get on.

As Derek sidled by me with the other kids headed for the van, he turned briefly and flashed a rare smile. His teeth were straight and white. He shook his head, half-laughing at me. "I'm gonna miss your skinny white ass," he said. And then he turned, got in the van, and I never saw him again.

5

As Long as We're Here

DESPITE THE POOR EXECUTION OF MY PADDLE WITH DEREK MASON, I did have some experience as a navigator of canoes. Dubious at best, but experience nonetheless. My dad was, and remains at the age of eighty-one, an outdoorsman with a voracious appetite for suffering. And yet despite that, he can be kind to a fault, and generous with his time and resources, even if the recipient of said kindness is a bedraggled offspring who approaches life with all the intent and focus of a deadhead enjoying a hearty meal of psilocybin mushrooms. There can be little doubt his stoicism can be traced back to his own Scandinavian parents and grandparents. As an octogenarian he still races bikes, competing in time trials and road races, and has crashed—spectacularly—many times, dislocating shoulders and hips and getting stitches in his head on a weekly basis. Case in point: When he fell a few winters ago skiing, he broke several ribs but *kept skiing with his friends* for a few runs. When the pain finally was too much for him to bear, he then—this is the part that astounded me—caught the shuttle bus to the hospital. No ambulance for him, god no. Public transportation would do just fine. His attitude toward physical discomfort has a nineteenth-century quality; I can imagine him biting on a musket ball while he amputates his own foot with a bayonet. And yet despite all this, his general bearing is an admixture of bigheartedness and candor.

When I was ten my father and I set out to canoe the New Haven River in central Vermont, where I grew up. The New Haven isn't a particularly big river—only a tributary to the larger Otter Creek—but it is a quick and rocky-bottomed little stream, winding its way down from the Green Mountains through the pastures, woods, and fields of Addison County until it joins the larger, slower creek. The sky was rainy. It had been pouring for days, though even at that young age I doubted very much that this would keep us from paddling the river.

My mother was concerned about the weather, about the danger the rising waters might pose. My father scoffed at the thought. We headed out the door, tying the canoe to our makeshift roof rack with bailing twine. We hustled and ducked, trying to hurry up and get in the car to escape the late spring drizzle that came misting out of gray skies. With our battered old canoe tied to the top of the car with frayed ropes and twine, we looked like Okies, the Joads on vacation or something.

We drove down rural roads, blacktop two-laners that were bordered by cow pastures, leaning barns, sagging double-wide trailers. Lawns with their rusted snowmobiles and mud-splattered ATVs.

Our plan was to put in upstream a few miles from our take-out spot, and then call my mother from some farm downstream to have her pick us up. The rain slicked our hair as we hauled the big, battle-scarred green canoe off the roof. I saw a slight hesitation in my father's face while we dragged the canoe through ferny and dripping forest to the bank. Water plunged and surged down the river, the color of tea from the mud sluicing down banks in the rain.

As I said, the New Haven is not a big river. But it was spring, and it had been raining for quite some time. Even the most benign little trickling stream can become quite rowdy with a surplus of precipitation, and that is exactly what happened with the New Haven. The narrow banks and thickly vegetated shores kept the water from spilling out, so it surged within this channel with surprising intensity.

My father looked up at the rain, back at the river. Back to the sky. Toward me.

"Well. As long as we're here," he said, and shoved the bow into the water, then handed me my kid-sized paddle. The current grabbed and tugged at the bow of the canoe. Getting into a canoe, which is keelless, is difficult in the best circumstances. There is simply no graceful way to do it. You place your hands on the gunwales, but put the tiniest amount of pressure on one side and the canoe obligingly rolls under the weight, which you then overcorrect in a panic by grabbing the other side, which of course rolls the boat back the other way. Meanwhile, because you're leaning out over the water with your legs still on dry land, your body weight is pushing the boat away from the bank, your body is getting stretched and you lose all leverage, so the only thing to do is awkwardly hurl yourself in the general direction of the canoe, banging your shins heartily and sprawling into the boat like a drunk being thrown into bed. The whole process is accompanied by small, breathy curses and grunts, and by the time you've embarrassed yourself fully and are in the boat, the only thing left on the shore—which is now drifting away—is your paddle and dignity.

When the bow is being hauled away by a surging current, it is that much harder. Somehow, though, I scampered in, banging and falling my way forward, the boat teetering violently from side to side as I made my panicked way to the bow. My father, without waiting for me to be settled, gave a violent, one-legged push against the slippery bank and grasped the gunwales in his hands. The boat veered out into the strong current, picking up speed immediately. We had a flurry of tight-knuckled paddling, as we both chopped violently at the whitecapped and heaving water as though it contained vicious piranha, to bring the canoe to rights and get it pointed downstream. My father uttered a series of contradictory commands, curses, and grunts. This was his idea of fun.

We began to find the motion of the current, switching sides to paddle on, getting the boat moving with a general bearing downstream. Much of our time was spent fending off rocks that stuck out above the water, pushing them hard with our paddles. The danger of rocks is that the bow will hit one and the boat will swing about, broadside to the upstream current, and thus be easy to capsize.

We got into a rhythm of sorts, though our rhythm was more like the drumbeat of an improvisational avant-garde jazz trio than a steady, four-on-the-floor rock beat. Now and then my father would tell me to employ a J-stroke, or some other piece of paddling wisdom. I'd listen politely and then go back to my lazy, noodle-armed stroke where I reached forward, dipped my paddle into the water, and let the momentum of the current glide my paddle back in what strongly resembled an actual pull through the water. On stretches of the river that were placid, we found that we could paddle well together, moving the boat with smooth speed. The rain had let up, and the banks were a tangled mass of green. We cruised past cows and trees and homes. Our trips were always in this vein—my father, goal-oriented and committed to the plan of whatever venture we were undertaking, whereas I was more like vaguely sentient luggage. Not unlike most teenagers. I was always a dreamy wanderer, sort of a spacey kid, and yet my dad would still willingly bring me along on these types of adventures, hoping perhaps that one day I'd come to and emerge from the fog of my own adolescent solipsism and become a fully functioning member of society.

We headed into a little draw in the river, which then boiled in a dog-leg turn of foam to drop off a bit more steeply. It was condensed, pitching whitewater here, but deep, and no rocks threatened. We swerved and pinwheeled back and forth, paddling and rocking. The nose of the boat dipped into a churning little drop, and I saw a large rock just beneath the surface off our starboard side. I leaned forward and lanced my paddle out, hoping to ward it off with a jabbing thrust. There was the grating sound of plastic on stone. A moment later, spearing my paddle back into the water, adrenaline coursing, I stroked and felt no resistance. Pulling my paddle out, I saw the wide, flat paddle part hanging, flapping, by a few strands of fiberglass. I'd broken the blade. I turned as the canoe pitched forward into the next foamy wash of river, one hand tightly gripping the paddle, the other now clamped on the side of the boat. Dad stared at my broken paddle shaft.

"Dad! My paddle!" My voice was high-pitched, a squeaky panicked yelp. I gripped the side of the canoe hard. My father stared straight ahead, downriver, looking over my shoulder.

"I got it," he said. His eyes were wide. He was bent forward at the waist, tensed.

The river at this point became difficult to navigate. Dropping off sharply into a steep rapid, it widened from bank to bank and got shallow. My dad now had to steer us through a veritable minefield of rocks—wet, black, cruel-looking things sticking up everywhere in the churning white-water. This was exactly the section where a bowman would fend off rocks, and the stern paddler steer. But I could only sit, neutered, and hope my dad would steer us through.

The sides of the canoe scraped against rocks, scratching and peeling away the thin fiberglass husk that kept us out of the water. I felt my scrotum shrink up until it was somewhere up by my kidneys at the thought of falling into this water that looked dark, cold, and tremendously uninviting. Then, as my dad paddled us through the pitching water, it began to rain hard.

It was nearly impossible for my dad to see to steer, with the splashing water and falling rain. Before long the canoe lurched, smashing and jolting as the bow crashed upward against a half-submerged rock. I screamed, grabbed the gunwales, and all conscious thought was replaced by animal panic. My dad tried to paddle furiously, hoping to power us over the rock. Our canoe rocked dangerously, then the stern caught in the current, and we began to be pushed sideways by thousands of gallons of surging water.

"Shit!"

The canoe flipped. The water pushed us over, and we rolled toward the water.

I fell headfirst into the icy shock of the river. I sucked in a big mouthful of water, rolling and spinning in the chaos of whitewater. I couldn't tell which way was up. I struggled, kicked, clawed out with my hands. Finally, my head broke through to the surface.

Dad was cursing and splashing about nearby, trying to get to the canoe by swimming after it through the whitewater that churned around us. The boat was now traveling quite easily atop the water minus its load, happily bobbing along upside down. Dad gave up, and motioned and yelled to me that we had to swim to the bank. We did, finally splashing to the edge of the river. We lurched over the slippery bottom, the current pulling us thrashing downstream, until we could purchase a foothold on the slippery, rocky bottom and force ourselves upright in the current, crouched and sliding about in waist-high water that tugged and pulled and kept sucking us downstream. Finally we were able to reach a little eddy that allowed us to get over to the rain-soaked bank, smashing our shins on rocks, and haul ourselves out by slippery, gnarled tree roots hanging over the river.

What followed was pure Laurel and Hardy. I could almost hear the jaunty piano accompaniment as we ran after the canoe, still caught in the current and heading out on a journey of its own. Slashing through banks grown reedy through spring, leaping over logs, we chased our overturned canoe as it lightly bobbed and floated down the river. Our water bottles and hats, bags, and paddles floated in its wake.

It's surprising that I continued outdoor pursuits as I grew up. Despite a great deal of evidence that I was inept, I kept sticking my nose into nature, intent on learning whatever lessons there were to be learned out there. There were many moments I had as a kid outdoors that taught me to love the wild, developed my sense of self-reliance, and helped orient the moral compass of my soul.

Boy Scouts was not one of them.

6

Superfly

THE CAMPSITES WERE ALL LOCATED IN A LARGE BOWL IN THE FOREST, a gentle circular valley shaded by tall maples. We'd hiked in with our local scout troop, arriving at the jamboree for a few days of wood-craft and scout lore. I had on my back my trusty external frame pack, a little beige number that I'd attached my tent and sleeping bag to with bungee cords. I had brought all the necessary survival gear: can-teen, Marvel comics, Garbage Pail Kid cards, and a trusty Swiss Army knife. Many of the other troops had already lit smoky fires in hastily assembled rings of stones and put up their tents, so from a distance the valley looked like an army encampment where all the soldiers were prepubescent. My fellow scouts hustled down to figure out a space to build our own little fire ring and set up tents, but all I could think about was getting down there and putting some poor screaming kid into a figure-four leglock.

I don't think the significance of the World Wrestling Federation in terms of aiding a budding sense of identity can be overestimated. Grow-ing up in the 1980s, the steroidal heroes of my youth figured massively in my imagination, both literally and figuratively. Hulk Hogan, "Rowdy" Roddy Piper, Mr. T, the British Bulldogs, George "The Animal" Steele—these slickly oiled, obscenely muscled entertainers were, to me, the per-sonification of cool. But none of these pituitary oddities held me in thrall quite like my personal favorite, Jimmy "Superfly" Snuka.

Snuka was a Fijian wrestler who raised the bruising art of wrestling-as-entertainment to the level of art with the introduction of his high-flying "superfly" moves. He'd climb to the top of a fifteen-foot cage around the ring and leap, body fully extended like a gibbon jacked on cocaine, and crush opponents. It was like watching a tiger pounce on prey, and to me, a young kid, it was the coolest thing I'd ever seen.

Perhaps seeing my obsession with Snuka and the WWF in general moved my parents to the decision; perhaps it was the hope of instill-ing some sense of civic responsibility and moral fiber. Either way, I was enrolled in Boy Scouts, where my love of wrestling would cause one of the most traumatic experiences of my young life.

I attended exactly this one jamboree during my short career as a scout. For the uninitiated: A jamboree is where multiple troops from a particular region all meet and camp together for a few days, dozens of young boys out in nature learning woodcraft and citizenship and how to avoid over-zealous scoutmasters.

There were no toilets or even outhouses where we camped in the forested valley. The scoutmasters designed and oversaw the construction of a latrine, which was simply a hole dug next to a fallen log a short walk from the main camping area. The process of using this ingenious setup was hideously pantomimed by one of the troop leaders. He imitated the act of dropping his pants, sat on the log with his derriere sticking over the edge, and walked us through how we'd deposit our contribution into the hole. A military folding shovel was stuck in the ground nearby; you covered up your offerings with a few scoops of dirt in an ineffectual bid to avoid mass E. coli–related outbreaks of dysentery.

The problem was that this arrangement became high entertainment for the scouts, who would gather to watch the unfortunate boy who chose to relieve himself, hooting and hollering in giggling, pointing knots of derision as the beet-faced kid grunted and tried to poop, meticulously recording the moment in minute detail in their hippocampus to relate to therapists decades hence.

There was no way in hell I was going to use that latrine. I felt it represented a dignity event horizon, beyond which I could never return to normalcy. I decided, as I walked back toward the main camp, that I would "hold it" for as long as necessary rather than subject myself to soul-rending shame.

I wasn't the only young boy obsessed with the stars of the WWF. Many of my fellow scouts also shared my passion for bikini bottom–clad giants, so we formed a "ring" made of fallen trees and took turns wrestling each other. This was great fun, and we even developed "tag teams" and had "managers," as the typical wrestling script called for sneak attacks by managers who clobbered unsuspecting wrestlers with folding chairs.

Soon we had a good group of kids playing. This was the 1980s, so adult supervision was practically nonexistent. Some of the older scouts were already surging with testosterone, and savagely thrashed us younger kids. Tears abounded. One brute, who looked for all the world like a grown man, hurled one kid down and stood over his wrecked body, sticking out his tongue à la George "The Animal" Steele. That was fine by me if he wanted to pretend to be Steele. I was adamant: I was Snuka. Other boys chose their own personas—"Macho Man" Randy Savage, King Kong Bundy, or André the Giant—but I, and only I, could be Snuka. He was my guy, and represented a kind of zenith of wrestling awesomeness.

Snuka's life outside the ring was ugly. In 1983 his girlfriend at the time, Nancy Argentino, was beaten to death in the George Washington motor lodge in Allentown, Pennsylvania. Snuka would be charged with third degree murder in 2015 for her death, but deemed unable to stand trial due to mental incompetency. In the final years of his life, Snuka suffered from various symptoms related to chronic traumatic encephalopathy, or CTE, which is the disease du jour for NFL players and wrestlers who spend years smashing their heads into each other.

Snuka was no saint, obviously. Addicted to cocaine and a heavy steroid user, the narrative of his life is painful to read. I knew none of it at the time. I was blissfully ignorant of his personal life, just in love with his high-flying, Tarzan-esque antics. I revered him far more than the most prominent star of the time, Hulk Hogan, who came across as this stereotypical American hero, do-rag and ridiculous mustache pointing toward a cartoonish male virility that I couldn't jibe with.

In 2016 Hogan filed a lawsuit against Gawker, a blog site that documented a leaked sex tape that featured Hogan. He was supported by Peter Thiel, a tech mogul and Donald Trump supporter. The lawsuit bankrupted Gawker. Perhaps as some kind of karmic payback, Hogan was outed during this period in recordings that have him using the N-word to describe his daughter's romantic partner. Sex tapes and hate speech. Classy guy.

It's always painful when the heroes of our youth turn out to be murderers, addicts, racists, and planetary-sized assholes. But in Vermont during the 1980s, that's what we had; it was either monster trucks or wrestling. So there at the jamboree, I helped organize a WWF-style smackdown and happily threw myself into the ring when I was tagged in, skinny body and all. As I wrestled—doing my best Superfly impersonations, leaping off the downed logs that stood in for the ropes—I began to feel a heaviness in my gut. It became intensely clear that the Boy Scouts menu of the previous twenty-four hours—which consisted of baked beans and instant oatmeal—was a force to be reckoned with.

I started running as fast as I could away from the other scouts. Sprinting into the forest, I wanted to put as much distance between them and myself, given their proclivity for turning bowel movements into a spectator sport. As I sped along, I miscalculated the timing, and in a moment I can only describe as sheer horror, it happened. I pooped my pants.

I stopped running, frozen. I hurriedly unbuckled my belt and slid my Lee jeans off my hips. My underwear was smeared. I didn't know what to do. I looked wildly around. Nothing. I began to waddle, contaminated pants around my ankles, through the forest, looking for something to use to clean myself. Hot tears began to well up.

To this day, whenever someone mentions the Boy Scouts, this is the image that comes to mind. Me waddling through the forest, soiled pants around my ankles, crying. I eventually found some leaves and cleaned myself up the best I could. And in a moment of what I can only guess was inspired by some deep sense of economy that my parents had instilled, I cleaned my underwear as best I could, then carried it back with me to camp and stuffed the offending article deep into my backpack. I don't recall if I was afraid of my parents' wrath if I had thrown it out, or if I was worried that leaving the underwear out in the woods would invite detection if found (how anyone would know it was mine I never considered), but whatever the reason, I stowed the smelly underwear in my pack and carried it around for the next few days.

When I got home at the end of my trip, I buried my backpack deep in a corner of our basement and quit the Scouts immediately.

Years later, when I was no longer a smooth-cheeked youth but instead a morose, zitty teenager, my father and I commenced a project where we poured a concrete floor in the basement, which until then had been dirt. Prepping meant cleaning out everything, and as we carried out old furniture and moldy, swollen cardboard boxes filled with the detritus of life, I never once remembered the backpack. Until, of course, I heard my dad say something to the effect of "Hey, your old scout pack," followed by "Gah!" barked in a tone of disgust. "Jesus Christ. What the hell's in your backpack?" I stared back at him in the gloom of the basement, my arms full of a broken lamp. Looked him straight in the eye. "I have no idea," I said.

The Scouts had not been a good fit. It wasn't that I had anything against helping old ladies across the street per se, but the whole thing smacked vaguely of militaristic fetishism. The hierarchies, uniforms, badges—not my style. I developed, early on, an appreciation of outdoor spaces as a way of eroding authority, of exploding hierarchies.

While I was still in high school, I devoured the requisite books that feed the wanderlusting soul—*On the Road*, *Leaves of Grass*—which did wonders for my imagination but wreaked havoc on my grades. As I reached my most surly teenage years, I became so enamored by the romanticism of the open road—a close cousin to the wilderness expedition in spirit and form—I thought the purest way to live, to really be alive, was with a rucksack and extended thumb, dusty boots headed down some lonesome highway.

7

Love and Abscesses

My adventures with kids like Derek Mason continued through the weeks. Later that summer I was between courses and stuck at the Scottsmoor basecamp with Pete. We were near the eastern coast, not far from Cape Canaveral. Stuck at the small ranch house buried in miles of orange groves. It was inland Florida summer hot—a furnace. The nearest store was a gas station about two miles away. Neither of us had a car. At first, the break from being on course was welcome. But as the days passed, I began to realize that being stuck in a house without air conditioning in central Florida is, in fact, the tenth circle of hell. Dante left it out of the *Inferno* after a legal dispute with the Disney Corporation, as they had copyrighted the tenth circle with the line to ride Space Mountain.

Pete and I spent our days in intense lethargy. We were the only two who happened to be between courses—there was no one else at camp. We had not been paid yet, and because of an unplanned (and unbudgeted) weekend of revelry down in the Keys the previous weekend, during which we drank our weight in large, slushy fruit cocktails and tented at a KOA campground, we had no money. None. Not even spare change. Until the next wave of instructors came—still a week off—we had to survive off unripe oranges pilfered from groves nearby, and whatever we could find in the musty, moldy basecamp pantry. We found only an oversized bottle of Kikkoman soy sauce. In the Eisenhower-era fridge was a big tub of generic cream cheese, two weeks past the expiration date and practically unused.

Nearby was a Vidalia onion field, vast, stretching for what looked like dusty miles. We harvested a bunch of onions and brought them back to basecamp. We ate them raw, like apples. We cored them, stuffed the core with cream cheese, doused the whole thing with soy sauce, and baked them. We lived off onions, cream cheese, oranges, and the hope that resupply would bring both food and our paychecks. Our flatulence—plentiful to begin with—began to smell like sour teriyaki sauce. The entire house took on a dense, unpleasantly stuffy stinkiness punctuated by the sound of trumpeting onion farts. It was deeply unpleasant. I found a few novels, and read and reread them sweatily on the couch, seeking any shade or cool breeze I could find.

One day, a dusty van pulled up. It was one of the logistics crew, who asked if we wanted to accompany her on a resupply trip out to a course that was in the area. Pete and I nearly sprinted to the van, desperate for any distraction. The van grumbled and chugged out along the two-lane blacktop edged endlessly in pine trees, and the sheer motion of the van and wind from the open windows nearly brought me to tears. After a few hours we drove down a rutted dirt road to a swampy boat launch shaded by cedars and slash pine.

Monica was two more years into her stint as an OB instructor than me. She was tall and broad shouldered with long dark hair, wide feet with splayed toes, and hands larger than mine. Her father, she told me, was Iranian. She hadn't shaved her legs since the eleventh grade and could handle the adolescent felons we worked with like nobody's business. She and her boyfriend lived in a pop-top Volkswagen van. He was bearded and long-haired and a black belt in Tae Kwon Do. They were the lead instructors on the trip we were resupplying.

I will admit here to having a massive crush on Monica. Now, this may have been because I was nineteen and so charged on hormones that I was known to get horny looking at JCPenney catalogs, or perhaps because I had spent so much time in isolation with Pete, who did not exactly get my juices flowing, but whatever the reason I found her backwoodsy, rough-around-the-edges brand of exoticism just what the doctor ordered. I quickly began acting like an idiot and embarrassing myself, as is the custom of young, inexperienced males the world over. Her boyfriend, who probably could've knocked my head right off my neck with a roundhouse kick or something, was just amused at my antics and, thankfully, resorted to simply ignoring me.

During the course Monica got an infection on her foot. A blister or a corn had become impacted, and she let it go until it was swollen and septic in the moist Florida outback. We realized that if it wasn't addressed, Monica would have to be taken off-course.

Some of us had just completed our Wilderness First Responder course. In a prime example of how reduced and desperate circumstances will make just about anything entertaining, Pete and I were dying to be the ones to deal with Monica's grotesquely swollen foot. She gamely allowed us to help, though looking back, I wonder why in the world we were trusted to attend to anyone for any injury more serious than a hangnail. Perhaps weeks in the swamps had made her question the validity of her life, and she saw this as a way to reaffirm her commitment to this mortal coil. Either way, she gave her assent, and once the kids were in their tents for the night, Pete, Monica's boyfriend, the logistics crew, and I gathered around with our headlamps trained on her foot.

Using rubbing alcohol, I sterilized my blade, a small clasp knife that was honed razor sharp. I used more rubbing alcohol to clean the area around the infection. The impaction was right on the ball of her foot. It was swollen and hot to the touch—there was dried pus and blood around a dark and evil-looking eye in the middle of the mound. I sliced gently around the head—Monica drew a sharp hissing breath—and pus immediately came seeping out. I made a half-circle incision, and then, using both thumbs, began draining the infection. The pus came out watery and cobwebbed with strands of blood at first, and then I got to deeper, older stuff the color and consistency of honey. I used my knife to trim the necrotic tissue from around the abscess. The bright light of my headlamp illuminated nothing but Monica's foot, and moths dive-bombed my head as I hunched over my work. The wound smelled, but we drained and cleaned it until no more blood or fluid came out. I trimmed all the dead tissue I could, and we bathed the area in rubbing alcohol. I remember finding the moment to be both utterly erotic and really, really gross.

I spent a stuffy night in a tent listening to Pete snore. In the morning the kids and Monica and her boyfriend got ready to paddle off downriver with the fresh supplies we'd brought. Pete and I boarded the van. Instead of heading directly back to basecamp at Scottsmoor, the driver, whose name I've long since forgotten, suggested we take a detour to a beach he knew of on the Gulf Coast side. We gamely agreed, with undiluted enthusiasm, as our only entertainment had been trading a waterlogged copy of a Robert B. Parker crime novel back and forth.

We arrived at the beach, a scrappy tidal stretch of broken mangroves, swampy inlets, and a few shell-scattered beaches. I waded through little inlets among the mangroves. Under the surface, the roots of the mangroves provided shelter for snook, gray snapper, and sheepshead. Above, cormorants and brown pelicans used the branches for rookeries. I saw from a distance a manatee's broad back stir the surface. I walked along the beach, caught in the kind of deep reverie that only the young and unencumbered can manage. With no kids of my own at that point, no real direction other than to be outside, I had access to huge swaths of imaginative landscapes. However, mostly I just tried to think of ways to get girls to talk to me. Futilely, I might add.

I had zero desire to head back to basecamp and wait to be picked up for my next trip. I thought I could explore the beach forever, finding weird shells and trying to spot manatees. I had no idea, then, the preciousness of that kind of time. How it would be forever before I could wander alone, along mangrove-choked beaches, dreaming of Monica's hairy legs.

8

Bittersweet Cowboys

It started raining our first night out. Shuffling off the road with heavy packs on our backs, guitars in hand, we made our way through the dark trees and found a spot in the woods to camp. Food planning had been haphazard at best; I believe we had Snickers and Marlboro Lights for dinner. As the rain soaked through our clothes and it became clear we'd have to bunk down in the woods amid the trees on the sodden ground, the exuberance that had buoyed our spirits quickly dissipated and was replaced with a gnawing sense that perhaps we hadn't thought this through.

There is a moment in every poorly planned outdoor adventure where the dynamic among the participants coalesces around a vehement and palpable resentment toward the person who planned the trip. It doesn't matter if it's on some fancy-schmancy bike tour of French vineyards and the foie gras isn't to your liking, or on an Everest ascent and there's not enough oxygen to go around. Someone is to blame. I have no doubt that as the Donner party descended into starvation, madness, and cannibalism, someone at some point had some choice words for the organizers. *See Jim? I told you. I said, "Maybe you should bring more salt pork." And you were all like, "Nah, one barrel is good." And I said, "You sure Jim? Maybe an extra barrel wouldn't hurt." And you were all sure of yourself. "Pffft! We'll be through to the coast of California in no time, surfing and eating oranges," you said. Well, guess what Jim? Now we're eating Clara. What do you have to say about that?*

Poncho and I eyed each other in the gloom, no doubt thinking about who would make the better meal.

In high school I was enamored by the idea of dropping out, hitchhiking across the country, starting a rock 'n' roll band, and living a sun-kissed, West Coast lifestyle replete with hedonistic excess. My friend Poncho and I made a plan to see this scheme through. We met early one morning on the docks of Burlington, Vermont, and took the ferry across Lake Champlain to New York, where we commenced hitchhiking west, making every attempt to embody the cliché of disaffected youth. Somehow, in my underdeveloped prefrontal cortex, I had combined my rudimentary understanding of the narrative arcs of Tom Sawyer and Huck Finn with the origin story of Guns N' Roses. Poncho and I both dropped out of school and ran away from home, leaving notes for our families and setting out into the wilderness to experience hardship and sacrifice in order to hone our creative spirits so we could arrive in California hardened and wise and write songs like "Welcome to the Jungle."

The band we'd formed was called the Bittersweet Cowboys, and we were the biggest band in our town. Actually, we were the only band in our town. Most of our song lyrics were thinly cryptic complaints about never getting laid. We completely bought into the mythology of rock 'n' roll origin stories. I had devoured books like *No One Here Gets Out Alive*, the biography of Jim Morrison, as well as *Appetite for Destruction*, the Guns N' Roses story, both of which were penned by Danny Sugerman. I thought that if we were truly going to achieve epic rock-god status, we needed to manufacture an origin story replete with homelessness, wanton drug use, and rebelliousness to the extreme. I thought a cross-country trip would do the trick. Hitting the road, I felt, was the way to expand our story, fill our quiver with the necessary experience to write rock ballads of unyielding beauty, and set us on track to sell out Madison Square Garden in a few years' time.

In retrospect, if I ever get to meet Jack Kerouac and Walt Whitman in the Elysian Fields, I've got a thing or two to say to them about the "open road."

It was a terrible night; the drizzle misted over us and got everything wet. We hadn't brought a tent, as we'd applied the same preparedness logic to our camping supplies as we had our larder. Poncho and I laid out our sleeping bags on spongy leaves, trying to scootch under the overhanging boughs of a large white pine. We resigned ourselves to misery and discomfort, grimly steeling ourselves for a long night. I tried to lie directly under a large limb above me, hoping that if I could shape my body exactly like the curve of the branch I could stay out of the rain. This futile exercise occupied me for quite a while, and surprisingly, I began to feel sleepy once the sugar rush from the Snickers had worn off.

We lay in the darkness for some time before we began to hear sounds in the forest around us. Rustles and chitters, squeaks and the unmistakable movement of some animal in the night.

Here I will admit to being scared of the dark. Even now, as I near the half-century mark, when I am sleeping in the woods at night, all rational thought departs. It's as though my mind gets wiped clean of all the logic and practical thinking I've accumulated, and is replaced by some primal caveman brain. When I hear anything, it's a bloodthirsty jungle cat coming to eviscerate me, never mind that I live in Vermont some three thousand miles from the nearest jaguar. I cannot help but have my colon clench up in terror when I hear the whisper of shifting leaves in the dark, and stare out blindly into the blackness of the forest at night, heart racing like a 1980s stockbroker on a cocaine bender.

I pulled out my flashlight, hands shaking, and switched it on. Wildly sweeping the beam back and forth, I saw that we were surrounded.

Prehistoric-sized raccoons stalked us, their lumpen, hissing shapes at the very far reach of the glow of our flashlights. *Git! Shhhhht! Psssst! Hey! Git outta here!* My voice had the shaky, reedy sound of a bedwetting child. Poncho and I threw sticks and made as much sound as we could, and finally, probably bored by our histrionics, the raccoons ambled off into the trees and left us alone.

At last, deep into the night, we were able to fall asleep. As anyone who camps regularly can tell you, the moment when you finally start to fall asleep, despite the physical misery and deep sense of regret you feel at camping in the first place, is one of the sweetest sensations ever. I began to drift, thankfully, into oblivion, sinking into my wet sleeping bag emotionally exhausted and spent.

I was soon awoken by the ground shaking as though we were in the grip of an earthquake. A shrieking, clanging beast came charging through the blackness toward us, an incandescent light burning our eyes and illuminating our pathetic little camp. We had unknowingly hunkered down close to railroad tracks, and an early morning freight shook us from our brief rest.

The night continued on in this way, small bits of uneasy sleep interspersed by bitter bouts of bone-weary wakefulness. Finally, the sun made a belated appearance somewhere in the sky, giving us enough light to pack our backpacks and begin tromping along the road again. We were silent as we walked, lost in our own thoughts. My own brain began to vacillate wildly between an almost sexual longing for waffles and a deep, creeping realization that I had clearly not thought through this whole *go west, young man*, Horace Greeley misadventure.

Finally, after what seemed a lifetime, the rain let up and left us tramping along the side of the two-lane blacktop deep in the piney woods of upstate New York. We were headed several hundred miles west to the campus of a college one of our friends attended, where we planned to stay the night. Thus far, our lack of luck hitchhiking suggested we might not make it, as we seemed to be the only humans slogging along the road in what felt like an endless, dripping forest.

Is there anything more dispiriting than hitchhiking on an empty road? The few cars that drove by did so at Mach speed, and otherwise we were left with the emptiness of the forest, the endlessness of the road, and the grime and sweat collecting under our pack straps. We passed a derelict motel of some sort, long since abandoned, and a makeshift memorial on a tree by the roadside where someone had met their end. Finally, the sun began to nudge aside the thick scrim of clouds that had been casting our adventure in gloom, and our spirits responded as well. Perhaps it was this infusion of spirit and joy that caused a beige pickup, finally, to hit the brakes after it sped past our thumbs and pull to the roadside ahead of us. Absolutely giggling with relief, we jogged up to the idling truck.

The man who got out of the driver's seat was smallish, with little mole eyes and rimless glasses. Dressed plainly in a T-shirt and jeans, he was maybe thirty-five. He offered to let us ride in the back of the truck in the open bed, a decision that probably made sense, as we had slept in the woods and smelled like it. We threw our packs in and clambered into the bed.

"Have you boys been saved?"

We both were mute, frozen on the spot. As a deeply committed sin-filled heathen, I have always responded to overtures of the biblical sort from proselytizers the same way I'd act if a large, rabid dog was in the vicinity: I get real quiet and try to fade away and make my escape. This time such a ploy wouldn't work, so I mumbled something purposely inaudible and hunkered down in the bed.

"Where you headed?"

"Next town," I said, eager already to get away from this guy. He nodded, and handed us both a pamphlet with a picture of Jesus and a lamb on the front.

"Maybe read this while you're riding."

He hopped back in the cab and we were off. We politely flipped through the little brochure without reading it, marveling at the speed with which we now crossed the landscape, having gotten used to the sludgy pace of sleep deprivation. Our clothes had the damp and funky smell of mold and body odor, and our stomachs grumbled with hunger. I felt, after only twenty-four hours, totally wrecked and fatigued. I was depressed that our grand tour, the adventure of our lives, was turning out to be such a bummer. Poncho lit a smoke and glanced again at the pamphlet.

"Well," he said. "If this is being born again, I kind of wish I hadn't been."

I smiled grimly, staring out at the trees as they whipped by at sixty miles per hour.

We only made it to western New York before packing it up and going home. Crossing New York east to west may not seem like much, but anyone who's ever made the drive from Albany to Buffalo knows the state is roughly the size of Mongolia and almost as bizarre. For example, we passed through Oneonta, a city known to have more bars per capita than any other town in the United States, according to urban legends.

We had all the requisite adventures. Met lost souls on buses and beneath freeway overpasses who smelled sour and sad. Grew to smell sharply sour and sad ourselves. Eventually made it to our friend's campus, where he was following a more practical route of education and gainful employment while we were intent on making or breaking it as a rock band. We stayed the night with him, sleeping on the floor of his room. I got savagely drunk the way only a seventeen-year-old can and spent the evening throwing up in the bushes. Most of the time was spent squatting by the roadside waiting for rides to emerge from murky forests, smoking and playing the part of the romantic wanderers.

We would head back home after only a short time, content to ride out our late teen years in the bosom of home, where someone else paid the rent and kept the lights on. We would go on to rock as hard as we could given our musical, financial, and cultural limitations—we played songs like "Mama Kin" by Aerosmith and "Every Rose Has Its Thorn" by Poison (no, I am not joking). We tried our hardest to be cool and use the cudgel of glam rock to smash our way to some understanding of ourselves. We were ridiculous.

I remember, though, the morning of our departure on the ferry across Lake Champlain. We stood on the deck, guitars in hand, backpacks swaying on our backs, as the ferry chugged across the slate gray waters. The dark line of forest on the other side began to slowly emerge into more detail, and the feeling I had—of impending adventure, of unknown exploits yet to come, of heading into the unknown with a friend by my side—it was one of the sweetest moments of my life. The sublime pleasures of the young and the clueless.

9
Ol' Stink

DESPITE THE POPULARITY OF THE BITTERSWEET COWBOYS, HIGH
school felt rather like a colonoscopy—a necessary though barbaric experience that doesn't quite seem to make sense. I graduated high school with
admonitions never to set foot there again from teachers, staff, and my
associate principal, who, in a moment that I thought painted a particularly ungenerous portrait of the odious little Napoleon, said as he handed
me my diploma with a mean, tight smile, "Didn't think you were going
to make it."

Before my time with Outward Bound, I headed out west to seek my
fortune. I worked at a ranch in Colorado with a group of degenerates
like myself. I had dreamed—abstractly—of living the open-range life per-
sonified by the *Lonesome Dove* novels of Larry McMurtry. I also blame
Steinbeck, whose books often portrayed the down-and-out as these noble
types, who by dint of circumstance may have been simple laborers or
farmhands but possessed some inherent goodness or wisdom. I bought
into that idea entirely, and wanted to live a life of hard work and sun, work
my body into a lean whip instead of going to college to become some
soft-handed peely-wally aesthete.

The official cowboys on the ranch I ended up spending a few months
working for actually carried guns—though they were typically automatic
pistols tucked in the waistband of their jeans rather than old Colt revolv-
ers—but I was not allowed to participate in any fundamental way in their
daily activities. I was, instead, part of the maintenance crew.

This was before the internet, and I had gotten the job by sending away
for tourism catalogs, ranching newsletters, livestock guides, anything that
might have the address of ranches out west. I applied to work at ranches
in Wyoming, Montana, Nevada, Colorado, Arizona, and New Mexico. I
was eighteen, and my previous work experience was, I thought, decent
curriculum vitae for working with cattle. I had worked in orchards, as a
dishwasher, as part of a landscaping crew. I had what I considered a bona
fide resume of the lumpenproletariat.

I desperately wanted to be a ranch hand. In fact, I had some experience with horses, as my family had owned a few when I was kid. When

I was still in elementary school, we kept a pony named Jewel in the lop-sided shack out back.

Jewel was bombproof. She could jump, though not very high; she could ride Western, English, pull a cart, a sleigh. She didn't spook. She was a fat little sausage of a pony, part Shetland, and mostly white with a faint pattern of little gray highlights. She was a hand-me-down from my sister, who rode hunter ponies competitively growing up. My sister was Vermont's state champion in equestrian events before she was even in junior high. I got Jewel for my very own when Kirsten moved on to a larger pony, a beautiful chestnut-brown mare—a mountain and moorland New Forest pony—named Green Mountain Honeysuckle. We called her Honey.

Unlike my sister, I was not a competitive rider. Or I should say that I competed, but was not competitive. In the standard events I entered, there were six kids from my region. All of us showed up early in the mornings to fairgrounds and horse corrals across the state, walking and trotting and cantering at the will of the judges who assessed our technique, form, and gait. I got sixth place—last—almost every time. First place was a large blue ribbon, second a red, third a yellow, and so on. Sixth was a green. My room was positively wallpapered with green ribbons, a verdant meadow of mediocrity. My sister's room was like a blue ocean.

There was one event Jewel and I excelled in: the "trail ride." You had to maneuver your pony through an obstacle course of sorts, stepping over hay bales, delivering a letter to a mailbox by riding close enough to lean down out of the saddle. We won first, and often, in that particular event (we fared better in the costume event as well—Jewel as Silver, me the Lone Ranger). We did well in trail riding because that's how we spent our time together. My father built a corral for my sister, who would practice jumping with Honey. But I had little desire, skill, or patience for riding in circles around the ring. Instead, Jewel and I would plod gamely around the fields and forests along Leicester Hollow, stopping to eat fresh green grass. We'd ride through dark pine forests, dripping water wetting my back as I ducked under rain-soaked boughs. We trotted up and down logging roads, Jewel's big steady hooves clip-clopping all the while.

Just as kids today seem to have forgone the childhood dream of becoming an astronaut, so too have they moved on from cowboy fantasies. I was part of the last generation of children who imagined themselves as lone, dusty riders of the pioneering trail. Raised on *Little House on the Prairie* and reruns of *Bonanza*.

I was drawn to the image of the cowboy, slouched in the saddle, staring out over a hard-baked desert plain. The reality, of course, was much different. Taking care of a horse is tough, and early morning slogs out to the paddock, with a heavy bucket of oats banging against my leg, were ammunition for plenty of whining. Plus, Jewel could be stubborn. She would sometimes just stop while we were out riding; arching her neck down, she'd crop grass, and no amount of hauling on the reins could stop her. She would eat her fill.

And so I felt—riding on my little pony, guiding her into a pond where she'd swim with me on her wide back, or galloping through a field—like I was a cowboy, that I was consistently working toward a life where "bedroll" and "leetle doggies" would be standard phrases in my vocabulary.

Jewel and Honey were loaded into our little trailer one summer day to head down to the Addison County Field Days fairground, a sprawling complex of livestock barns, horse corrals, exhibition buildings, and bare patches of earth that held the agricultural fair. There was a horse show that day, and Jewel and I were to be in it. The sky was dark with clouds; it felt like rain.

The first event I was scheduled to be in was "show," a kid's version of dressage. The goal was to make horse and rider look as smart as possible. I was confident Jewel and I were about to fail miserably. I was slovenly, and Jewel, though a great little pony, was not known for her sharp looks or stately bearing. She was a hedonist who overate and looked it. She loved a good roll in the grass or mud, kicking her four legs up in the air and reducing her hair to a dirty, dusty carpet snagged with bits of straw, burdocks, and mud. Jewel would permit us to groom her—to be rubbed vigorously with a curry comb, beribboned and glossed until she shone—but it wasn't in her nature to be haughty. She was a grubby work pony meant for the mucky heath and boggy lands of her Shetland side.

But I was resigned to participate in the competitions. I started braiding her tail and mane with my father and mother's help. My sister was already warming Honey up, looking quite the English lass in her blue blazer with shiny brass buttons, jodhpurs, and high, black boots. I wore my standard riding outfit of a checkered shirt, jeans, cowboy boots, and a nice, white, high-crowned cowboy hat. I finally got Jewel looking presentable and headed corral-side to watch my sister ride in the hunter pony competition. She really was a marvelous rider, balancing on the balls of her feet, heels down, as Honey leapt over jump after jump. My sister leaned out, stretching over Honey's neck as she cantered around the ring. Horse and rider working together—horse's ears forward and eager, rider poised and balanced—is a beautiful thing to watch. As I admired my sister riding her way to another first-place finish, I feared that Jewel and I didn't quite cut so fetching a figure. I had a feeling we looked dumpy, silly, as we bounced along—straw-thin boy atop fat pony. Uncoordinated, slouching ruffian riding surly work horse.

But perhaps it would be my day of redemption. I walked back toward the barn where I'd left Jewel contentedly eating hay an hour or so before.

Jewel, small as she was, had plenty of room in her stall. She must've gotten an itch—one of those you can't quite reach, up between the shoulder blades in the middle of the back—and decided to scratch. She dropped and rolled, no doubt loving the crispy, fresh scrub of sawdust that was heaped on the floor as she twisted and rubbed, grinding her broad white back into the earth.

There were several piles of fresh, steaming, green road apples in the stall. Jewel had rolled right over them, smooshing and painting herself with her own turds. There was now a big green stain of horse manure on her shoulders, back, and sides. She didn't even look guilty, eyeing me afterward as she munched her hay.

Thunder grumbled as my parents and I set about furiously scrubbing her all over again. We used towels, brushes, swatches of hay—whatever we could. Not only did the green stain of manure cover her white hide, but she had embedded untold thousands of particles of sawdust in her hair, mane, eyelashes, and tail.

We did the best we could—got her looking nearly as smart as she had before she rolled, then hurried out toward the show ring, the announcer's tinny, staticky voice announcing the lineup for my event. As he read off our names and the names of our ponies, we rode in one by one. The event was a stupid one, I thought, because all you did was file in, make a couple of circles, and then stand there, beside your pony, and get ranked on how clean and well-groomed you both were. Something in my boy's nature rebelled against this judgment every time.

I stood holding Jewel's reins in the center of the ring. As the thunder boomed overhead, a light rain began to fall as the judges walked officiously around me and my competitors, all of whom looked a sight better than I. My parents and sister watched from the stands, crowded with all the other families and horse people hurriedly snapping open umbrellas and donning coats.

The rain began to produce a curious effect on my little pony. Shetlands have coarse, thick hair, bred over generations to withstand the freezing wet chill of the wild and stormy north seas of Scotland's coast. As the rain began to soak Jewel, a large, amoeba-shaped green stain began to appear. The rain's effect on the manure, which had been ground close to the skin, was to bleed it out, make it run, and change the hue from the brownish, earthy olive of horse turds to a lighter, more effervescent and verdant color.

Jewel turned leprechaun-shit green as the judges eyed my pony with evident curiosity.

I looked at the ground, my face hot with shame. And my felt cowboy hat, with its high crown and sharply turned-up sides, disgorged the reservoir of water that had collected on it, spilling down in a neat little waterfall onto my muddy cowboy boots.

Jewel died a few years after that, and I never really rode horses again. But I still remember the mornings I spent with her. I would stand in her stall, warming myself by leaning my whole body into her bulk. Back then I could practically walk right underneath her without bending over. I'd hang out with her, eat the same oats she ate, right from her bucket. On cold mornings she'd bow her head, closing her eyes, and I'd stand directly in front of her, with her big long forehead against my chest, warming my frosty hands in the hollow crook of her throat.

Of the dozens of ranches I applied to, only one offered me a job. Horton's Ranch, a tourist destination dude ranch, in the high country around Gunnison and Crested Butte, called me and offered me a job as a bike mechanic. But only if I could repair bikes. The conversation is one that would be echoed throughout my life as I gained access to jobs I was completely unqualified for through the delicate and pervasive use of outright lying.

"Can you work in our trail bike repair shop, helping ranch guests with their bike rentals and ensuring the bikes are in good condition?"

"Absolutely."

"Do you know how to repair bikes?"

"Absolutely."

I had no more idea how to repair a bike than perform triple bypass surgery. But they offered me the job, and off I drove in Mr. Basic, my little car so named because other than the engine and steering wheel, the car offered little in terms of amenities. My thought was that I would start out repairing bikes, and once I was entrenched in the organization, I would transfer to working with the horses, buy boots and hat and gun, and live out my cowboy dream. The entire issue of actually knowing how to fix bikes would be solved on the job, I decided. Actual preparation would be far too time consuming.

When I arrived, it became abundantly clear that I was not going to fix bikes. Whether they saw through my lies, or decided that my resume suited me better for less sophisticated labor, I was assigned to maintenance.

I pulled into the ranch parking lot after a few days of endless driving, Mountain Dew, and peanut butter and jelly sandwiches made on the dashboard of Mr. Basic, and turned off the engine. I got out and stretched, long and languorously, looking around at the ranch. I saw a bunkhouse in the paddock with the horses. I could hear the lowing of cattle, and saw the lean figures of men in cowboy hats over by a horse barn. Scrubby, sage-covered mountains rose all around me.

A large guy in his twenties approached me from what looked like the main building of Horton's Ranch, enclosing the general store and a restaurant. He wore a beaten, dusty, leather cowboy hat. It looked authentic. He was obviously working on a large wedge of chaw, and spit accurately and professionally into the dust of the parking lot, never taking his eyes off me. I introduced myself, and his smile seemed friendly enough.

"Y'allwunt sumptin' ta et?" he said.

I am from New England, and though Vermonters can have some pretty thick woodchuck accents, I thought that maybe this guy was foreign, from some place I only knew about in theory, like the Baltic region.

"Excuse me?" I said.

"Y'allwunt sumptin' ta et?" he said again.

Ah, right. Did I want something to eat. It turned out Jeff, who I had mistaken for a flinty-eyed, six-shooter-slingin' ranch hand, was actually a Southern-fried frat-boy volleyball player from the backwoods of South Carolina. He was to be my counterpart on the maintenance team, and I would spend ten hours a day with him over the summer.

Jeff showed me around the ranch that first night. I met everyone except the head of the maintenance crew, Mike, who Jeff informed me was "sleeping it off." I assumed "it" meant a hangover. I would later discover, though, that in order to be hungover you must first be sober, a condition I never observed Mike in during those three months.

Jeff was a handsome enough guy, tall and broad in the shoulders, with blue eyes and the sort of tousled surfer hair that you see on every poster in American Eagle and Billabong advertisements. He was gregarious to the extreme, popular with the other staff, and on good terms with the ladies, to whom he was courteous, innuendo-heavy, and apparently very enticing. He was also—and I say this at the risk of condoning a stereotype of southerners, which is not my intent—an abject racist. He broached the subject with me that first night as he showed me the stables where the actual cowboys kept their gear.

"Y'all got a lot of Black folks where you're from?" he asked.

"No, I'm from Vermont. Hardly any," I said.

He considered this. Turning to face the breadth of the ranch in the fading light of day, he seemed contemplative, as though the strange and ill-formed thoughts of others would always be a mystery to him.

"People around here say I'm a racist. But I ain't. I just hate Blacks and Jews," he said.

The logic of this, I must admit, rather escaped me. But, considering he was in possession of a .357 magnum handgun with a six-inch barrel, which he had shown to me on the tour of the bunkhouse, I decided to say nothing and store that bit of wisdom away in my "why Jeff is crazier than a shit house rat" file drawer I had just hastily constructed in my head.

Mike, our boss, would drink a mixture of Mountain Dew and Southern Comfort all day, and dip tobacco and smoke cigarettes at the same time. The man was a walking carcinogen. He had a three-legged dog he'd found feral somewhere out in the canyons around the ranch, and named it Ol' Stink. We sometimes knocked off early for the day, a process Mike would always initiate by looking wan and thirsty and saying, through his tobacco-stained mustache, "Well, it must be five o'clock somewhere," and when we did, sometimes Mike treated us to Ol' Stink's talents.

There were a number of cabins on the property for guests, mostly Texans, to stay in. Oftentimes, due to the foundationless nature of the structures, various animals burrowed into the cool, shaded areas under the cabins and made homes there. Most frequently, these squatters were feral cats. Mike would bring Ol' Stink out to a cabin with the feline interlopers, and he'd get the dog all riled up and ferocious, and then set him on the cats. The tripodal canine would fire off into the hole under the cabin, where the most god-awful shrieks and hisses could be heard. Mike and Jeff would chuckle and laugh as Ol' Stink ripped apart the cats under the cabin, and I would try not to vomit and stand there feeling out of place and very dandified, like Oscar Wilde at a NASCAR race.

Ol' Stink, it should be noted, got his name because one time a similar escapade was initiated and it turned out not to be feral cats, the males of which have a spray that can be rather skunk-like, but the actual article itself, a skunk, that Ol' Stink ripped to bits. And it was true, though I was informed that this skunk killing had happened years prior, the smell of it clung to the little heeler, and whenever I dared to pet the googly-eyed dog, my hand would come away smelling like putrid skunk glands.

This job of maintenance involved some of the most horrific labor-intensive tasks I've ever had to endure. One was patching the horribly pitted and potholed little roads that ran through the ranch. Jeff would shovel smoking-hot blacktop patch from a wheelbarrow into a rut or hole in the road, and I would tamp the steaming pitch down with a seven-foot length of fence post. Oozing pitch and full of splinters, the pole weighed practically as much as I did, beanpole that I was. We never got to switch jobs, and as I stood there breathing in the toxic fumes and tamping the holy Christ out of the black and oily patches, my shoulders would burn and my lower back felt like it was full of broken glass. Due to the code of male stoicism, however, I dutifully completed my job, and at the end of the day would get ice from the mess hall and soak my blistered, aching hands.

One of the more unpleasant aspects of the job involved garbage. All the garbage we collected ended up in our own private dump on the property, a shallow hole out of sight of the paying customers. All the garbage, that is, except the food-related kitchen garbage, which Jeff and I would put in a twelve-by-twelve-foot shed so it wouldn't be torn apart by critters. We'd empty the shed once a week. Imagine the leftover bones of fried chicken, gravy and biscuits, plate scrapings, eggshells, all the stuff of a kitchen left to rot and simmer in the high plains Colorado sun in the middle of summer for a week. When we had to haul the thirty or so bags, once a week, to the town dump, it was a brutal experience.

My first time performing this task was memorable. Jeff and I drove the dented and battered maintenance Chevy truck to the on-site gas tank, where we filled a little five-gallon container and put it in the truck bed. We then drove the bouncy and rutted road to the horse pasture, where the dump shed was. Jeff got out of the driver's side, I the passenger, and we stood together in front of the shed.

"Go ahead and open it up. Ah'll git the gas," Jeff said.

I opened the latch on the shed. The smell was ripe and bad just outside with the door closed, but when I opened it, the reek was incredible. Fat, garbage-glutted flies by the hundreds flew out in a swarm and slapped clumsily trash-drunk against my face; they felt like hairy airborne grapes. The smell was overpowering, a hot wave of rot. I could see the whole mass of bags almost vibrating as they seethed and ballooned in the sweltering confines of the shed.

I lurched to the side, stumbling away, trying to draw air into my lungs that wasn't fetid and stinking.

"Pretty goddamn awful, ain't it?" Jeff said.

Jeff doused the pile with gasoline to help with the smell. The fumes from the gas, plus the heat of the shed and the reek of the garbage, made it hellish to hoist the wet, slimy bags from the ground and hurl them into the truck. The first one I tried was heavy with god only knows what, and as I tried to quickly lift it up and toss it into the truck, it smashed against the tailgate and splashed and spilled hundreds of trash-fed maggots all over my bare arms. I turned aside and threw up so hard I ended up dry heaving in the dust while Jeff laughed.

We rode into town to dump the trash, my head a swollen, noxious balloon from the fumes. Jeff happily drove, chewing a wedge of tobacco. I remember dully questioning, in the part of my brain that hadn't been completely erased by inhaling fossil fuel vapors, why we used gasoline to cover up the smell of rotting garbage, as it seemed both wasteful and expensive, but mostly I hung my head out the window and tried to gulp in huge breaths of dry air.

"You gonna stay fer winter?" Jeff asked. The manager of the ranch had asked a few of us if we wanted to stay on past the tourist season. Keep the pipes from freezing, plow the driveways. Run the boiler and shovel snow. I looked over at Jeff the racist. Glanced back at the swollen bags of garbage flapping in the open bed of the truck.

"Maybe," I lied.

10

Gazing into the Abyss

Our first night on the trail was a rude baptism. We spent the day skinning up to above the treeline, a few of us pulling sleds packed with food and gear as well as wearing our heavy backpacks. The altitude was a killer, as was the weight we pulled. My muscles were jelly within minutes, my breath a high-pitched whistle. We were soon high up, and as darkness fell, a swirling snow complicated things as we set up our first camp, the Rockies looming around us. I wondered, in a woozy, hypoxic kind of way, how exactly I'd ended up there.

Before heading down to Florida to begin training as an instructor, I'd taken a few Outward Bound courses myself as a student. I'd briefly attended a fancy prep school for a second senior year of high school in the hopes of resuscitating my flatlining GPA and go to college. Once deposited in a boarding school at the tender age of eighteen, I smoked bales of marijuana, snuck booze into my room for parties, and confirmed every stereotype possible for an entitled white kid from New England. I got put on probation for "cruising," what we called sneaking around at night outside the dorms. My defense—that hallucinogenic mushrooms are best enjoyed outdoors—fell on deaf administrative ears. It wasn't long before I dropped out and showed up on my dad's doorstep, unkempt and unenrolled. Eager to be rid of me, my father sent me off on a couple of Outward Bound courses. He enrolled me because he felt it would be an excellent way for me to develop independence and self-reliance, and toughen me up. Also because I think he was worried that if he had to look at my tuition-wasting face any longer he'd smash it in with a large object like a brick or a Cuisinart.

I arrived in Colorado via Greyhound in March, and was shuttled up into the Rockies to join our ragtag group—a few younger folk, such as Evan, a kid close to my own age, as well as some more-adult attendees, including a producer for daytime soap operas from New York. All of us were either between phases in our lives or looking for some kind of adventure.

After our first day of hauling sleds up steep mountainsides through neck-deep snow, I was given the responsibility of digging the latrine.

Basically just a hole in the snow we would cover with a couple of feet of hard-packed snow when we shuffled off in the morning. I gamely dug a trench well out of sight of camp.

That night, after a classic wilderness meal of some gooey stuff resembling spackle mixed with old bubblegum, I found myself in need of relief. Thanks to my cross-country Greyhound journey, several days of road food, bad coffee, and lack of exercise had created an intestinal traffic jam of massive proportions, and an afternoon of skiing had done the charitable deed of moving things along the agenda. As the temperature dropped in the darkness of the Colorado high country, I put on my headlamp and shuffled off through the trees to take care of business.

I was faced with a number of challenges. First of all, three layers of pants—long johns, fleece, and large, Cordura nylon pants that Outward Bound provided to students. I gingerly edged backward to the side of the hole and began wrestling with the bulky layers to pull them down. Given my over-the-ankle mountaineering boots, I couldn't get the large wad of clothing pushed down very far—it was all bunched up behind my knees. And I had stupidly dug the latrine too far away from any helpful trees that would've provided a sturdy handhold.

In order to pull off a successful enterprise, I had to lean way over, awkwardly sticking my rear over the pit while keeping my balance on the edge. My muscles were burning from the day's ski with pack and sled as I assumed a masochistic contortionist's pose like I was performing in some scatological Cirque du Soleil. The wind blew, and gritty bits of snow blinded me as I bared my backside and tried to gently ease myself into position over the hole.

Trying to relieve oneself while straining every single muscle, in the dark, over a pit in the snow, breath ragged from eye-popping altitude, all while wrapped up in layers of fleece and nylon and polypropylene, headlamp beam bouncing wildly around, wearing a pair of mountaineering boots, nether regions shrinking from the cold—the whole project was doomed from the start.

I managed to fire off the first few rounds, but my legs were trembling. Balance was precarious, and the shifting snow under my feet and near darkness gave me little to no visual cues to my body's position.

At some point my momentum went past whatever razor's edge only physics can determine, and I began to fall into the very grave I'd dug for myself. It was while I was peeing, so as I fell, awkwardly twisting, a lively stream of urine whirled about like a lawn sprinkler. I tried to arch my body, roll—do anything to avoid landing squarely beneath me. I failed. The fall was quick and the landing painless—physically, in any case, though my dignity was forever gutted. I believe I screamed a combination of words that sounded something like "*Gahsheetargew!*" to express my revulsion and shame.

There was nothing for it. I had to haul myself out of my own excremental grave, bare-assed and simpering. After scrubbing my body blue with cold, grainy snow trying to clean myself, I hobbled back to the tents, feeling defeated and tired.

"What took you so long? Train not arrive on time?" said Evan. He was smiling. I wondered if I could trigger an avalanche to fall on him the next day.

11
Solo

Boredom is the dream bird that hatches the egg of experience.
—WALTER BENJAMIN

ONE OF THE MOST DISTURBING FACTS ABOUT CAMPING AND SPENDING time in nature is that there is no television. No internet, either. While this may not seem obvious to those who haven't spent time exploring the wilderness, to those of us who do know, it is nothing short of horrifying.

When I took my first Outward Bound course, it was a twenty-one-day ski mountaineering adventure in the Rockies. I spent those three weeks stomping around snow-covered mountains, dragging sleds and skiing, and learning to avoid avalanches, build snow caves, and develop my soprano singing voice as I took "snow baths," a hygiene method that involves scrubbing your body with snow, which both cleans you and removes any chance of an erection for nearly six months.

On this trip I had the opportunity for a two-night solo. This is a tradition in Outward Bound where the people on the trip stay by themselves, isolated in the wilderness, surviving only on peanuts and raisins while the instructors head back to basecamp and eat steaks, drink beer, and watch reruns of *The Simpsons* in footy pajamas. Making people pay to leave them alone in the wilderness is, in my humble economic opinion, the most brilliant business strategy of all time.

So there I was in the high country of Colorado, camped out alone in a snowy pine forest. I wanted to be organized, so I planned to spend the first few hours getting all situated. I dug my little tarp into the snow, created a nice compact sleeping platform inside, and organized my gear. Then I looked at my watch and saw that exactly fourteen minutes had gone by, and the realization that I would be spending nearly forty-eight hours by myself without so much as a book to read set in.

I remember lying around napping quite a bit that first afternoon. I counted the raisins I ate one by one, then the peanuts. I'd drink an entire Nalgene of water in one go, just so I could pee later and have something to do.

Generally, I'm about as self-reflective as lichen. But with all this time on my hands, I thought back to how I'd ended up in a little blue tent by myself surrounded by hundreds of square miles of snow-packed mountains.

A few months earlier my dad had signed me up for the course. As I mentioned, he was no doubt eager to be rid of me and my self-absorbed moodiness after my second epic academic dropout. He sent me west to clear my head, and in an attempt, I believe, at redirecting a tendency toward self-destruction. I drove out west in an Isuzu on palliative care that gave up the ghost somewhere near Erie, Pennsylvania, the engine seizing and the rusty SUV stalling to a dead stop on the side of the freeway. I walked to the nearest pay phone and found a local mechanic to tow it back to his garage, where he announced it dead upon arrival. I sold it to him for $100 and jumped on a Greyhound.

Riding "the dirty dog" is truly the last great and relatively affordable way to stop your life and take a look around. As the bus trundled across the frozen fields of a gray and icy March, through Pennsylvania into Ohio, across the vast ice-locked fields of the Midwest, my adolescent wheels were spinning. I brought Tolkien's *Lord of the Rings* trilogy and read the whole thing through. I ate really terrible food: gelatinous eggs coated with filmy grease and safety-vest orange cheese; slices of gas-station pizza where the dough was uncooked and the pepperoni had the texture of freshly removed scabs; microwaved egg and sausage sandwiches that struck uneasy truces with my gag reflex and would slosh around my stomach for hundreds of miles.

I began, after the first day on the bus, to adopt a curious odor. I'd never smelled quite like this before, I thought. This was the smell of guys who lived deep in subway tunnels.

I arrived at the Denver Greyhound terminal in the early morning. I had a few hours to kill, so I wandered around downtown, stopping in at the famous Brown Palace Hotel. My dad had told me to check it out. I went into the empty bar, ordered coffee, and sat there feeling hollowed out and grimy. Over forty-eight hours on the bus, no shower, malnourished by the vitamin paucity of America's highway and byway provender. The bartender, in his black vest and bowtie, looked me over as he stocked the bar with ice and glasses, preparing for the early lunch crowd. I had, at this point in my life, tried to grow my hair long à la Kurt Cobain. It hung greasily down my head. I wore flannel and ripped jeans with patches. Thank you, grunge movement, for forever inhibiting my sense of polish. The bartender regarded me with a queer mixture of concern and disgust.

"You look like shit, kid."

"Thanks," I said.

I was picked up a few hours later at the appointed spot in a large white van that had "Colorado Outward Bound School" written on the side. The driver was Mark, who would be one of my instructors on the trip. His humor was infectious, and everything he said was with a lilting, jovial, self-deprecating air. I liked him immediately, and he, to his credit, did not immediately classify me as a drug addict due to my overall appearance.

We began the long, slow drive up to Leadville, where the Outward Bound basecamp was located. The other folks on the trip were a motley crew: Dave, a balding, bespectacled accountant who had "never done anything like this"; Jane, a producer of daytime television; Carl, a guy from upstate New York who lived off a huge severance package he'd received from some corporation; Jake, a snowboarder in his early twenties; Marlon, a young guy from Baltimore; and Evan, who'd been relegated to the trip by family members and, I suspected, some kind of court diversion program.

I had often thought that if I had to make a living, I would try to do so outdoors if at all possible. Perhaps a professional skier who was whisked around the globe on private airplanes to star in movies or perform stunts for James Bond films, or maybe the Discovery Channel would give me my own show where I'd wrestle walruses or something. But the suspicion that I was doomed for a life of itinerant outdoor employment was confirmed when I met Tahoe. Tahoe was the senior instructor on our twenty-one-day ski-mountaineering course. Compact and muscular, he was about five foot six. His nose resembled a squashed and beaten loaf of bread. His eyes were intense and wide open. His face had the bronzed and craggy look of someone who spends a lot of time in high-altitude sun. A shaggy goatee completed the look of this tousled mountain man, who instantly, in my mind, became the dog musher from Jack London's *Call of the Wild*,

Perrault. Swarthy and small, wizened and quick. He was irreverent, funny, out of touch with popular culture to a pathological degree, and generously kind. I wanted, in the ways only a teenager in the throes of hero worship can, to be him.

The trip was a disaster—half the students ended up quitting halfway through. But for me, it was an epiphany. Despite it all, I had fun. I loved being outdoors, cooking with melted snow. I loved the effort it took to get from one place to the other, and how after a while it wasn't that hard to drag a sled and ski with a pack on my back. Evan was struck with snow blindness. One night he awoke from sleep and couldn't see, freaked out, jumped up, and ran smack into the wall of the tarp-tent, tearing a gap in the wall. Tahoe would sometimes scream in his sleep, and I would hear Mark calming him down in the darkness. Every time he woke up, Mark told me, it was because he had a dream that he'd been buried in an avalanche. Tahoe's other job was as a guide on Denali in Alaska. He'd been in avalanches twice and lived, so the nightmares were horrific replays of what had actually happened.

The guy from Baltimore, Marlon, suffered some sort of back injury after about a week and a half of skiing. We had to evacuate him—emptying one of the sleds and heading back to basecamp with Marlon strapped tight to the bottom of the sledge. The night we got back to basecamp, Carl, Jane, Evan, and Marlon all took off in the middle of the night, leaving the trip midway through. Marlon had faked his injury, or at least the severity of it had been fake. They'd had enough, and left the trip.

So it was just a few of us out there enjoying our solos. As the afternoon crawled painfully toward evening, I tried taking another nap. I thought resting up before I ate more raisins and peanuts would be a good strategy.

I'm not exactly sure when and how the solo became a fixture of Outward Bound's philosophy. I'm guessing it had something to do with surviving the mental extremities of being lost at sea or stranded alone, though clearly all you need to do is make friends with a volleyball. But it was tough, to sit there, with your own thoughts, for that long. At the age of nineteen, I had zero ability to be self-reflective.

By the second night I was in rough shape. I'd already eaten all my raisins and peanuts, and drunk about one hundred gallons of water so I could pee as often as possible. My campsite was crisscrossed with little paths I'd created wandering around. I'd started talking to myself, a non-stop monologue that consisted mostly of catchy one-liners from 1980s action movies. *Hasta la vista, baby. Yippee-ki-yay motherfucker. Adrian!*

It was my birthday. March 29. I'd mentioned it casually to the group, but pretended like it wasn't a big deal. The fact that I was spending my nineteenth birthday by myself fit neatly into the narrative of self-imposed suffering I'd adopted as an adolescent. My calculus was that if girls felt sorry enough for me, they might let me get to second base. This plan never actually worked, but it didn't keep me from creating situations that made me seem pathetic.

As night fell, I sat in my darkening tent, feeling bad for myself. A birthday, and there I was, drinking lukewarm snowmelt out of a dirty Nalgene bottle with no food left. I began to consider giving up, when I heard the swish of skis approaching. I climbed out of the tent, and there were Tahoe and Mark, skiing up to me. Had I somehow stayed out for two nights already? Had my sense of time become so out of whack that I had lost track of the days? They were grinning ear to ear.

"Happy birthday, mate," said Mark. He handed me a Pepperidge Farm chocolate cake. He and Tahoe then skied away, leaving me with an entire cake in my hands.

I sat down immediately in the snow and began shoving fistfuls of cake into my mouth. I have had intercourse, seen the birth of my child, and witnessed the glories of this universe. But none of them compare with eating Pepperidge Farm cake in the snow.

That trip was the inspiration. A few short months later, I'd go through instructor orientation and then work for Outward Bound in Florida with juvenile offenders like Derek Mason. Eventually, I headed out to the West Coast, where, after a hot second as a Hollywood script reader (I was terrible; I panned the script for *Scream*, a film that went on to gross $173 million, clearly demonstrating that I had absolutely no showbiz acumen whatsoever), I began running trips in the mountains and deserts of California.

12

Death Valley

The desert, any desert, is indeed the valley of the shadow of death.
—JOAN DIDION, *SLOUCHING TOWARDS BETHLEHEM*

TRYING TO PREPARE FOOD ON THE SUMMIT OF TELESCOPE PEAK WAS like trying to cook in the backwash of a jet engine. Only cold. I hauled out my little camp stove, and, in the shelter of some rocks, finally got some water boiling for a starchy, carbohydrate-laden specialty I liked to call "cheddar risotto"—instant rice covered in dehydrated cheese powder. At one point, banging about in the darkness, hunched over like Gollum to avoid the wind, I put my gloved hand down on the still white-hot stove. My glove melted and burned, and the heat singed right through to my palm. A stifled scream was heard by none thanks to the hurricane-force winds.

Somehow, during the lighting and fueling process, I spilled the fuel for my cookstove. It pooled in the little nook in the rocks I was huddled in. I must have inhaled the toxic vapors the whole time I was cooking, because as I got up to serve the gloopy, cheesy mess I'd made to the students I'd brought up to camp near the peak, lights exploded in my head. I felt nauseous and woozy. I was just able to serve the kids their food before practically falling over, head swimming from the fumes. My vision blurred, my balance faltered. I thought I might pass out, so groped my way back to where my gear was stuffed in a crevice in the rocks.

I found, as I lay just a bit away from the kids in the darkness, that I had burned a large hole in my jacket as well, at some point resting it against the stove. My little kitchen area reeked of fuel and burnt nylon. I stuffed some crackers in my mouth for dinner and in the vague hope I could quell the urge to vomit, and spread my sleeping bag in a brutal cleft in the rocks to try to sleep.

It's said that George Mallory quipped "because it's there" as his reason for climbing Everest, and that profound response has since been used to explain space travel, plumbing the depths of the ocean, and eating the Awesome Blossom at Chili's. What's often omitted is that Mallory *died* on Everest, which deflates the existential logic of his most famous epigram.

In a way, however, I understand what Mallory meant. The whole Mojave Desert region held a certain fascination for me as a native New Englander. The road to Death Valley from Los Angeles winds along the Owens River. A dry, hot region bordered by the Mojave Desert and the High Sierra, the valley has been the stage for gold prospecting, cowboy movie backdrops (John Wayne was a frequent visitor to the town of Lone Pine to film Westerns), and fiercely pitched battles over the ownership of the water that flows through the Owens. Driving through the desiccated air on the way to Death Valley, I could taste dust on my tongue, the sweet tang of desert yucca, piñon, and sage. The ground is rusty and broken, cracked and burnt like some gigantic pottery mess left too long in the kiln. It's otherworldly, quite simply, and I wanted the students to experience that, the remote desolation of the place.

The late nineteenth and early twentieth centuries saw a huge movement toward the conservation of wild lands in America. This movement was led by famous cranks such as John Muir, but was often bolstered by the moneyed, white elites of the era. In terms of preserving the deserts of Southern California such as Death Valley, J Tree, and Anza Borrego, Minerva Hamilton Hoyt stands out as a leader among the early desert conservationists.

Born on a Mississippi plantation right after the Civil War, Hoyt married a wealthy physician and finally settled in Pasadena, California. After her husband died, she became a crusader for saving the deserts, as she felt automobile traffic and development were wiping out the natural landscapes. Her reasons strike a familiar chord with anyone who's visited these places: "The desert with its elusive beauty," she wrote, "possessed me, and I constantly wished that I might find some way to preserve its natural beauty."

She became a soldier in a campaign to save these natural spaces, traveling across the country exhibiting desert flowers and cacti, and knocking on the doors of elected officials to try to convince folks of the necessity of preserving these majestic landscapes.

In Hoyt's writing, as well as the words of contemporaries like Muir and other early conservationists, the natural world gets represented as this tabula rasa, a pristine Eden that needs protecting. "Nature's peace will flow into you as sunshine flows into trees," Muir wrote. True enough—I've had plenty of moments that feel pretty groovy when I'm out and about in the very places Hoyt and Muir worked to keep safe from development, agriculture, sunburned dirt bikers, and off-road enthusiasts. But in all the beautiful writing by these folks, all the soaring rhetoric, the erasure of the Indigenous peoples of the deserts and mountains is so complete, so absolute, it is easy (and a privilege) to hardly take note of their existence at all. Reading about these early enviro-warriors, it becomes clear what they wanted: to preserve beautiful places for the enjoyment of white people. Muir practically comes out and says it: "Thousands of tired, nerve-shaken, over-civilized people are beginning to find out that going to the mountains is going home; that wildness is a necessity." He's literally describing me, a stressed-out suburbanite in need of some woodsy balm.

The grim fact is that these incredible landscapes were made available first and foremost by removing the native peoples who lived there. I've spent quite a bit of time in my life in the High Sierra; Kings Canyon and Sequoia National Parks; the deserts of the Mojave, J Tree, and Death Valley, as well as East Coast wild areas such as the Green Mountains and Adirondacks. My own enjoyment, the very lifestyle I not only value but that constitutes a huge part of my identity, rests squarely in the reality of the disenfranchisement and genocide of native peoples. These vast, pristine tracts of land were not empty. They were populated by diverse peoples and cultures, had a human history stretching millennia before Patagonia puffy jackets and wicking layers. And this isn't ancient history. Native peoples still living around J Tree, for example, include the Cahuilla, Chemehuevi, Mojave, and Serrano. Unceremoniously kicked out so that white dudes like me could rock climb and hike and snap selfies.

The legacy of white monopoly of wild spaces is a tough one to navigate. The erasure of native peoples has been so obscenely complete that rarely is a second thought given to the ancestral occupants of the land. Sometimes, at best, some well-meaning liberal will acknowledge they are visiting native lands, but it's a nod, a brief mention, followed by a figurative emotional shrug. What can you do? Whenever the reality of Indigenous genocide, institutionalized dispossession, and theft is brought up, the reaction is the same. Us white people purse our lips, furrow our brows, and shake our heads in remonstrance of the sins of our ancestors, like a mother pooh-poohing her naughty child for some minor infraction. Then a big sigh, and it's on with the business at hand. After all, *what can you do?*

These incredible places where I've found so much joy are now managed and regulated by the very government that 86'd Indigenous peoples in the first place. Death Valley was once part of the lands of the Timbisha Shoshone, a desert-dwelling group that eked out their existence among the Panamint mountains and dry deserts. When the government tried to develop a homeland for them, they hired a designer known for his sensitivity to Indigenous peoples named Billy Garrett. The Timbisha Shoshone rejected his plans, not for some aesthetic principle, but because the process of approving the plans and getting permits was *too bureaucratic.* That remains the true evil, I think, of the way in which native peoples have been usurped of their birthright homelands. White power structures aren't always racists in hoods with burning crosses. Sometimes, they're hidden in plain sight in the monotonous inertia of institutions, molding the landscape to their desires and self-perpetuation. That's as scary as any trail of tears.

Telescope Peak is an 11,331-foot peak only a dozen miles from Badwater, the lowest point in the continental United States at 282 feet below sea level. It is said that the elevation gain from Badwater to the summit of Telescope Peak is similar in scope to the rise of Mount Everest as it juts up from the Tibetan plateau. When driving into Death Valley, visitors could get a sense of the dramatic rise of Telescope as it rose majestically from the desert valley floor.

The great central rift of the eponymous park is a low-lying, incredibly arid desert that receives barely measurable precipitation each year. It is not a place that welcomes life, though life in myriad forms stakes out a tenuous existence in a place that reaches summer temperatures of over 120 degrees Fahrenheit. Only a six-hour drive from Los Angeles, the park is enormous, but a drive down into the inner areas brings the dedicated visitor to a region that is like some strange Martian landscape scooped up and dropped in California. I wanted the kids to feel that dislocation you only get in hard-to-reach places, a place of no-placeness that makes you search for something in your interior geography to orient yourself.

We visited in December, the only time the temperature is bearable. The sky was an achingly beautiful, cloudless blue. The area around Death Valley—the Mojave Desert, the Panamint Range, the White Mountain Range, as well as the Sierras to the west—represents an incredible panorama of reds, whites, grays, and browns, like a massive earth-toned set of crayons had been used to color the landscape. You'd be hard pressed to find a more complete collection of burnt umbers and beiges anywhere else in the world.

Death Valley National Park is home to the largest wilderness area in the lower 48 states. Exempting only regions in Alaska, there is nowhere that is more remote, desolate, and empty than Death Valley. If I was looking to give the kids a wilderness experience, I had chosen the right place.

The father of one of the students had wanted to come with us. I had initially planned for just myself and another teacher, Ned, to lead the trip. But the man was insistent. He was a big guy, rotund, with long motorcycle-guy hair, like a linebacker past his expiration date. A gruff demeanor. His daughter, Gabrielle, no longer lived with both her parents; she lived predominantly with her mom. I could see that the dad was trying to use this trip as a way to bond. A way to spend some time with his girl, who was a full-fledged adolescent and came with all the concurrent eye-gouging frustrations that brought.

We'd set out from the bottom of Telescope Peak with high hopes. It was warmish even though it was winter, in the sixties. We'd driven in and camped the first night at the base of the trail right by the parking lot, thus able to take advantage of cooler-food like hot dogs and chips and sodas. I noted early on that Gabrielle's father, Mike, wore a leather jacket—the classic black motorcycle zip-up worn by badasses since Brando in *The Wild One*. I had given him the same gear list I'd given the other kids, which focused on light, outdoor gear. Windbreaker shells, down jackets, fleece, not a lot of cotton, the usual outdoor adventure stuff. His jacket alone looked like it was ten pounds of dried cowhide and metal.

It's a vital skill to wake early on rigorous mountaineering trips to ensure that you get all the daylight possible to traverse steep, technical ascents. At least that's what I've heard. I've never been good at getting kids out of camp early and hitting the trail to begin racking up the miles. I'm a lounger. I wander around in a stupor, packing, then repacking my gear, eating pancakes, drinking a fourth cup of coffee, admiring the view, scratching myself, and just enjoying the deaf ear and blind eye nature turns toward bodily noises and effluent.

But hit the trail we did, around mid-morning. Mike was hurting from the get-go. He overdressed right away, not realizing that lugging a pack was the fastest way known to humankind to raise your core temperature. His backpack was a geographical feature in and of itself, as it appeared to contain enough gear for Everest and a small sofa to boot. The thing towered above his head, stuck out on both sides, and was strapped and wrapped with various bags, random gear, and hiking doodads. He looked like he was being buggered from behind by a garbage heap.

If there is an outdoor equivalent to the Myers-Briggs personality test for children, it's trekking in the high country. They start out fast. The real go-getters race up the trail, bouncing along and talking loudly, shattering any hopes that fellow outdoor enthusiasts might have of bird watching or meditating. The speedy, energized ascent only lasts about seven minutes, and soon the kids are sitting on the side of the trail, complaining about one of three things: hunger, weather, or boredom.

Then there's the other contingent of kids who start slow and grumpy, know they won't like it from the start, and maintain a consistent barrage of well-thought-out arguments about why it's a dumb idea to go backpacking. I can't help but have a soft spot in my heart for the complainers. They are so steadfast, so true to their creed. The sheer *commitment* they show to grousing about hiking is admirable. I've had some kids who complained nonstop on eight-day trips.

On one particular trip I brought my wife along as a co-leader. I was leading the kids off-trail to demonstrate orienteering skills (outdoor instructor talk for being "lost"). My wife, who had been bringing up the rear with the complainers, came bounding past me, face set and grim, her hands quivering with rage. "If you don't go back there and shut those little shits up, I swear to god I'm going to kill someone," she said, and marched off down the trail.

The two kids in question were video game–addicted, suburban idiots who had been eager to take advantage of the fact that my wife had ears so they could pour every last syllable of whiny, bitter complaint into them. Eventually, she just couldn't take it anymore, and stormed to the front of the group.

We continued the slow climb up Telescope Peak. The kids spread themselves out along the trail. The route was carved into the side of the mountain; any attempt to leave the path would have hikers scrabbling up a forty-five-degree slope of broken shale. Telescope Peak is a classic climb in that it's monotonous and markedly un-fun.

Mike began to look worse and worse. Altitude can affect anyone, and most who ascend beyond ten thousand feet feel some effects: headache, nausea, dizziness. Altitude sickness resembles a hangover. Once up in the mountains, it never seems all that bad till you hoist your pack and strap it on at eight, nine thousand feet, then start climbing a trail reminiscent of Satan's Stairmaster. You notice it then. Your posture begins to resemble your eighty-year-old grandmother, and little spots have an annoying, blackfly-like habit of dancing in front of your eyes. Your breath is ragged and raspy, and conversations, sentences, words are often left half-finished and unsaid. Thinking becomes groggy and spacey. Sort of like being really, really tired and stoned, but with none of the endorphins. Mike was struggling, and I knew I had to do something.

"Mike, you want me to take some of your weight?" I asked as delicately as possible. His sunglasses had slid down the sheen of sweat on his nose, and his long hair was coming out of his ponytail and was plastered to his cheeks. His jowls were quivering with each hard-fought breath.

"We, *huh, huh*, close?" he asked, gasping.

"Ah, no. We've gone about a half mile," I said. He gave me a look that said, in very plain and clear terms, that I was an idiot. I faded back and let him be.

By noon we'd barely gone two of the eight miles needed to reach the summit. We slung off our packs in a saddle along a ridge, hunkering down out of a strong chill wind. We broke out our food, stuffing our faces with whatever didn't require cooking. The enthusiasm of the group had definitely diminished in an inverse relationship with the views, which were becoming more and more epic the higher we went. "Just look at that," I said, extending my hand, gesturing to Mars-like mountain ranges of red and scarlet that undulated to the horizon. The kids stared at me with undisguised hatred.

After a brief pause we began to get moving again. The kids groaned and complained, and I'm pretty sure I heard the phrase "child abuse" more than once. We all shouldered our packs and started up the trail. Mike still sat, legs splayed clumsily about, looking exhausted.

"Hey, Mike. I can take some weight," I said, waiting for his daughter to be out of earshot to save him the embarrassment.

"This wasn't what I expected," he muttered, his voice low and accusatory.

"Sorry about that, Mike. It's just, you know, we try to do these more rigorous trips to help the kids push themselves."

"I know why you do them," he growled. Our relationship, fraught to begin with, was deteriorating.

The day got later and later. The trail got steeper. The route up to the summit was a classic traverse, with the trail zigzagging up the face of the mountain. We soon reached the altitude where only bristlecone pines grew, and the wind blew unabated from whatever Pacific storm that birthed it. It got colder and colder, and kids began to whine with a particular panic in their voices. I sent Ned along with the faster group to make the summit, and I hung back with the laggers, who soon consisted only of Mike. He seemed to get that he was dragging the whole group down.

"You, *huh, huh*, go on, *huh, huh*, ahead. *Huh, huh*, with the kids, *huh, huh*," he wheezed. He did not look good. The kids were my responsibility, but now I had to factor in this guy as well. I was honestly concerned about him blowing a cardiac gasket on the trail at some point. I knew that if I left him to his own devices, the chances were good he wouldn't push himself out of guilt. He would go at his own pace, maybe even just stop. Which was fine, as long as he didn't die on me. I had a spotless record as far as death on trips was concerned, and I really didn't want to break my streak.

"I'll be back to check on you," I said, and hiked on up the trail toward the kids. Night was coming. Ned was up ahead, and I passed the kids, who were strung out along the mountain, and finally, after an exhausting jog up the trail, caught up with him for a consultation. We decided to get the kids to drop their packs; Ned would grab the stuff for the shelter and head up to the summit before nightfall. There was no place to camp where we were, only a narrow goat path along the steep mountainside. We could take turns ferrying the packs up the rest of the way once we got the kids settled. The kids gleefully dropped their packs, bringing only their headlamps and sleeping bags, and followed Ned up the mountain. This all took some time, and so I raced back down the trail, leaving my own pack, to check on Gabrielle's dad.

I found him looking despondent, sitting on the ground, leaning against a tree. He resembled a huge pile of spilled laundry.

"Mike, hey man. How are you? Doing okay?" I bent to look at him closer. He still wore his sunglasses, though we were in the shadow of the mountain, and his lower lip was trembling from either cold or exhaustion.

"This. Is. Bullshit," he said. I wasn't quite sure what he meant—his lack of experience, the whole notion of backpacking, maybe the human condition? I was pretty sure a debate was not what he was looking for.

"Mike, I'm going to carry your pack for you, okay? That way we can get you to the top. Kids are already up there. Ready?"

He lurched to his feet, and I took his pack. It weighed slightly less than a Buick filled with pudding.

We struggled up the trail together, though without the pack's weight, he seemed able to make it. I noticed one of his knees was severely knocked, and wondered what sort of chiropractic nightmare I'd just induced in this 240-pound man.

By the time we reached the summit, it was basically dark and the wind was screaming. The summit of Telescope Peak is a short little ridge. The camping spots are small, rock-ringed ovals, often just big enough to contain a sleeping bag or a one-person tent.

I had, in my zeal, and with the understanding that it only rains once every thousand years in Death Valley, omitted tents from our packing list. My theory at the time was that we could spread out on the ground, stare up at the desert stars, and experience a transcendent moment of natural serenity. What I had not counted on was that the altitude and howling winds would drop the temperature precipitously. What I had thought would be an excellent character-building experience was quickly turning into a dumpster fire.

Ned and the kids were crouched in the lee of rocks, trying to avoid the knife-edge of the wind. Ned eyed me skeptically.

"I probably should've brought a tent," I said.

I got Mike to one of the little hollows and helped him pull out his sleeping bag. His face was pale, and his pulse rapid. He looked like he was coming off about a weeklong bender. He took off his boots and climbed wearily in, fully clothed, like some large butterfly in reverse, if butterflies resembled the singer Meatloaf. The wind whipped by above his head, but lying down in his little hollow, he was out of the worst of it. I left him and scurried back to Ned and the kids.

The kids were huddled behind a rock wall, only about two feet high, that someone had once constructed. Ned was digging a tarp out of his pack. The kids were genuinely scared, and the temperature was dropping fast.

We worked together as quickly as possible, securing the tarp as a shelter to get the kids out of the wind. It was growing dark, and the temperature was now decidedly uncomfortable. The kids were rather mute, their reptilian brains kicking into gear and directing them to dive into their sleeping bags and conserve heat. The wind was picking up, and gusts blew around us.

This was when I tried to cook a meal for my charges and ended up huffing camp stove fuel and nearly asphyxiating myself in my little rock cleft.

Sleep was not to be had. I was so sick from the fumes, and trying to sleep in my little crevice was like trying to sleep in the jaws of a backhoe. I felt like it was breaking me apart just to lie there. I wrestled with my bag, climbed out, and checked on the kids, who at least were fed and packed together warmly at this stage, playing with their headlamps and farting and giggling, oblivious of the horrors nature was inflicting on us.

Headlamp beam bouncing around, I headed out to find Ned. I might have glimpsed the firmament wheeling overhead, showering us with the Milky Way's radiance, but I was so ill from the gas fumes I just scuttled over the rocks. I slipped and scrambled across the ridge as the wind sliced into me. Iridescent blue-white patches of ice shone in my headlamp's light.

I found Ned hunkered in a small site just below the branches of a bristlecone pine. He had his own little stove going, with a hot, steaming brew of miso soup just beginning to simmer. He had hung his headlamp in the low branches of the bristlecone pine, giving his little windless pocket a nice, warm glow. He had a small cutting board and paring knife, and was chopping fresh kale. A bowl of couscous and dried beans sat ready to add to the soup. There were some aromatic spices in tiny, lightweight plastic jars, and between Ned's knees was a hot, steaming mug of what looked like freshly brewed chai tea with real milk.

"How was dinner?" Ned said amiably, humming some happy tune. Not about to be dragged down by such pleasantries, I thought I'd bring Ned back to reality with some sharp words of reproach for neglected duty.

"Mike, he hasn't eaten yet," I began.

"Oh, I brought him some food," Ned said.

I faltered. Ned smiled pleasantly, and then bent back to his now-ready miso. I grumbled something about checking on the kids, and shuffled back along the deadly path to my own frozen coffin. I had carried Mike's lumbar-impacting backpack up the hill, and he got the gourmet macrobiotic meal prepared by Mahatma Gandhi. I wedged myself into my sleeping bag and tried to sleep through the nightmare night ahead.

Dawn came blue and freezer-burned to the top of Telescope Peak that next morning. A weak light poked out from the mountains to the east, illuminating the steely sky. The temperature was extreme, to say the least. I felt like one of those mummies *National Geographic* features seemingly every other month, all frozen and twisted and warped and stuffed into rocky crags in the Andes.

I wasn't dead, though it seemed a viable option at that point. I clawed open my pack and pulled out some food, anything, to feed the kids. My hand throbbed from the burn I'd given myself the night before, and the fuel I'd inhaled left my head feeling bloated and ballooned. I pulled some oranges from my pack that were frozen solid as rocks, and a Hershey bar or two for the kids to split. Just moving out of my sleeping bag was excruciating. The wind cut like a knife and howled into the hole I had burned in my jacket the night before. I scuttled over to the bivouac where the kids lay and peered inside.

Clearly, it'd been an uncomfortable night for all. Some were shivering, others passed out still sleeping. There was a rime of ice coating the inside of the blue tarp, and more than a few pairs of eyes stared at me with wide, uncomprehending shock.

"Is it morning?" one of them asked. I looked into her eyes, glad I could finally deliver some good news.

"Yes. It's morning. We'll start heading down soon," I said.

I've never seen kids so eager to leave a place in all my life. They all just maniacally gathered their gear, or most of it, and took off, arms full of backpacks, yelling frantically about getting the hell off this mountain. I was alone, picking up the discarded items they'd left behind, shivering in the dawn. Soon I was joined by a well-fed and rested Ned, who helped me break down our bivouac. I headed down, teeth unbrushed, stomach grumbling. About a quarter mile down the trail, Ned and I remembered Mike. We dropped our packs.

We found Mike tucked into his sleeping bag, still fully clothed, snoring peacefully. The bright sun of dawn had yet to wake him. His jowls quivered slightly with each long snore.

"He looks like a little baby," Ned said. I had to agree. It was so peaceful sitting there with Mike as he slept, the way a sleeping whale would be peaceful. Instead of waking him, we sat on the rocks and watched the sun rise over Death Valley.

13

Ready for My Close-Up

STEELY JAW. ICE-BLUE EYES. THE KIND OF TONED AND TANNED GOOD looks that make the masses swoon. A perfectly frayed cowboy hat, ringed with tarnished silver buckles. An assured, panther-like gait. Sex appeal. That was Mike.

Teaching in Los Angeles means that eventually you'll run into someone from Hollywood. Actors and stars are all over the place, and some of them are in breeding programs designed to produce perfect-looking children. See Gwyneth Paltrow and Chris Martin, Brad Pitt and Angelina Jolie, Will Smith and Jada Pinkett Smith. Their progeny need to learn to read and write and calculate royalties, and so teachers end up educating the celluloid elite. When I lived in Los Angeles I taught the children of famous authors, cinematographers, studio producers, actors, musicians—you name it. But the one I remember most clearly is Mike, an aspiring actor, ruggedly handsome and totally clueless.

We were in Joshua Tree, California, a mecca of rock climbing. A couple of hours from downtown Los Angeles, the park eponymous with U2's greatest album is a beautifully weird place. Huge dun-colored quartzite boulders are spread over the landscape, some in massive conglomerations like mountain ranges, others singularly sticking out of the sandy desert like Easter Island heads. It looks like some galactic rabbit had dropped its sandy turds across the world. The hard, gritty rock is perfect for climbing, and the park has thousands of recorded routes.

Situated at the confluence of the Mojave and Colorado Deserts, J Tree has an ecosystem all its own. The actual tree the park is named for isn't even a tree but a plant that can grow to forty feet tall. Spiky and twisted, early Mormon settlers thought the tree looked like the biblical Joshua raising his hands in supplication. But then, Mormans *would* think that, wouldn't they? Perusing the literature on J Tree, words like "weird" and "bizarre" and "alien" pop up frequently. It's all a matter of perspective. I'm guessing local Indigenous folks like the Serrano, Cahuilla, and Mojave who were pushed out of their homelands by waves of settlers (such as the pareidoliac Mormons) didn't find it weird or bizarre. It was just home. But plenty of interesting people had been drawn to the area.

In 1973, Gram Parsons, late 1960s counterculture musician and narcotic inebriate, died of an overdose at the Joshua Tree Inn. A former member of the Byrds and the Flying Burrito Brothers—still one of the all-time greatest band names in the history of rock 'n' roll—Parsons was a big fan of J Tree. He spent quite a bit of time there, particularly in the area near Cap Rock, a famous jumble of boulders smack-dab in the middle of the park, with the jaunty eponymous rock slightly tilted atop the dun-colored mound.

Parsons was a dubious but effective docent for J Tree, bringing the likes of Keith Richards (Rolling Stones, duh) and Michelle Phillips (The Mamas and the Papas), among others, to visit the park. The story of his death and the aftermath only adds to the bizarre history of the region.

His backstory is tragic. Both parents were alcoholic; his mother died of cirrhosis of the liver in 1965. After his family disintegrated (his father cheated on his mother when Parsons was still a kid), he turned to the salvation of music, inspired by an Elvis Presley show he attended in Florida. Parsons is credited with fusing country and rock together, drawing on various influences to create the pastiche musical form of Americana. If you hear a twang in a pop song, you have Parsons to thank. He is credited by music historians as inspiring Keith Richards to explore country music, and the two were friends, often living together and trading riffs and songs back and forth—actually, probably handing other substances back and forth as well.

But that creativity and lifestyle came with a price in the late 1960s and early '70s; Parsons was known to take huge amounts of drugs. Apparently, Parsons was quite the party boy. He was hardly picky; barbiturates, morphine, alcohol, LSD, and cocaine were all game.

That fateful September in 1973, Parsons was partying down in Yucca Valley and elsewhere. According to legend, he drank enough tequila to kill a buffalo and then met a random woman at the J Tree Inn who injected him with morphine. He passed out, and his fellow partygoers attempted to revive him with an ice cube suppository, which, when I personally imagine it, would likely wake me from the dead, but did not have the hoped-for effect for Parsons. He eventually stopped breathing and died.

Here's where things get very weird. Parsons didn't just enjoy J Tree; he loved it and felt spiritually connected to the place. In this way, though I've never passed out from morphine and had ice cubes stuffed up my butt, I feel a sense of kinship with the Flying Burrito Brother. Apparently, Parsons had previously asked friends to cremate him in the park upon his death. Though his body was taken to Los Angeles after his death, his road manager, Philip Kaufman, and a friend of Parson's, Michael Martin, stole the body and brought it back to J Tree, where they tried to burn the coffin and its contents near Cap Rock. J Tree employees brought the ceremony to an unceremonious halt when the smoke was spotted. The guilty parties were fined $300.

I was with a group of students, a few other teachers, and a handful of parent chaperones. It was always an odd recipe of people: Teachers felt scrutinized by parents as they harangued the kids; parents, seeing their child fully engaged in the social milieu for the first time, came to all kinds of self-absorbed realizations about their child; kids acted out in ways they'd never normally consider if it was only their teachers. Camping in this format is like living in a quirky village where no one is sure who's in charge and everyone is watching everyone else to see what they're up to. It's not terribly unlike middle school itself, just replacing adolescent awkwardness and self-consciousness with adult obliviousness and self-regard. It's a bit of a goat rodeo, really.

When I took students to J Tree, we'd top rope climb. Top roping is when there's a fixed anchor at the top of the climb where the rope runs through. The belayer—the person on the other end of the rope from the climber—feeds out line or reduces slack as the climber wedges and pries themselves up the rock. It's the safest way to climb, generally, and I'd start every morning by stringing a few routes. I and the other teachers would then spend the day belaying kids up and down routes, getting sunburns and sore necks as we squinted skyward to watch students clamber upward.

This particular day I had anchored three routes along a huge face of rock near one of the roads that winds through the park. Kids explored the area around us as they waited for their turn on the different routes. All morning, the desert echoed with the call-and-response of climbing.

"On belay?"

"Belay on."

"Climbing."

"Climb on!"

The sun soared across the sky as morning turned to afternoon. We'd picked a north-facing wall to stay shaded, and as the sun sank the shadows deepened around us. My goal was to get each kid to try all three of the routes by day's end. We were wrapping up, and, despite the fact that taking two dozen kids climbing is the organizational equivalent of herding meth-addled cats, we had some moments to spare. I offered the parent chaperones a chance to climb if they wanted.

"Do it, Dad!" said Topher, Mike's son. "Toph," as we called him, had the same electric blue eyes as his father, and possessed an unearthly athleticism. Put a basketball in the kid's hands, and he could weave through defenders like a scythe through grass. He was a force of nature on the soccer field, able to put on bursts of speed and move with a cougar-like agility that made your jaw drop. Just his raw speed and grace were something to behold. His parents crowed about his physicality— dreaming, no doubt, of a future career as a professional athlete/model/energy supplement spokesman. I heard through the grapevine, years later, that Toph took all his latent physical grace and preternatural abilities and fell in love with . . . screenwriting.

Mike squinted up at the wall from under his boutique cowboy hat. He looked like the Marlboro man, only without the cancer. His perfectly square white teeth gleamed in the shadows of Joshua Tree.

"Come on, Dad!"

I imagine many parents have been in this situation, both moms and dads. Your kid wants you to do some feat or act of intrepid bravery, like leaping into frigid water at the beach. Heck, *you* kind of want to as well, but can't find the gumption. You're also aware how freighted the moment is, how your kid is seeing you, in the world, attempting a challenge. You worry that if you back off and chicken out, you'll be deflating your child's parental reverence, ruining their life as they model their own apathy and quitter attitude on your own reluctance to hurl yourself into the void. Someday, you imagine, when they're homeless and eating a dinner of foil wrappers and roaches, you'll come across them hunkered down on a bed of old Ikea packaging in the street, and they'll look at you with woeful eyes and say, "It all would've turned out different if you'd just jumped."

Mike was not going to let him down. As a former male model, he understood the importance of image. Earlier that school year I'd had a parent meeting with Toph's folks. Mike had regaled me with a tale of his weekly pickup basketball game in Los Feliz (a neighborhood near Hollywood). He said Topher had wanted to come with him, to "watch his dad stud out." I'm not sure what "studding out" looks like, or, really, what it is, though it makes me think of horny stallions pawing at sawdust in a stable. But he wasn't joking or being lighthearted; he was using the phrase "stud out" in earnest. Since then, I've had aspirations of "studding out" myself that, sadly, have gone unrealized.

Topher's mother was a ghost writer for celebrities. She'd sit down with them and record their life stories and package it up in nice narrative chunks, minus the drug addictions and divorces unless they were framed as challenges and struggles that helped them find Jesus. She'd also written her own self-help book, *A Charmed Existence*, which detailed the lives of a group of celebrities and tried to offer the reader lessons for a better life based on their trajectories. I believe there may have been a chapter on cheekbones.

Mike was game to try a route. I asked if he'd ever rock climbed before.

"No," he replied. I began the same talk I gave to every new climber, but Mike waved me off.

"I got this," he said.

Taken in the abstract, rock climbing seems ridiculous. I mean, yes, you can *try* to climb vertical slabs of rock, but why *would* you? What's the point? It's a question I've asked myself as I've gotten older. I didn't question it when I was just heading out into the world in my twenties. I didn't question anything, really, as that required a certain level of self-reflection and analytical awareness. But now I get it. Yes, it's a weird act to contemplate, weirder still to do: risk life and limb climbing straight up big towering walls of rock, jamming your fingers into minute cracks and wedging your toes into shoes two sizes too small. But it does provide life with meaning. A certain *joie de vivre*, if nothing else. When you think about it, anything we do besides eat, sleep, and procreate, when taken in the abstract, seems bizarre. For example, we send older adolescents away to live in buildings, eat bad food, drink cheap beer, and listen to people who've read a lot of old books talk about stuff for four years, then we decide they're "educated." After that, we encourage them to go find a place with people that will tell them what to do, and, if they do it, reward them with little green slips of paper. They can then exchange that paper for lamps from Crate and Barrel, or pretzels, or more beer. We call this having a "job" and being a "grown-up," but really it's all pretty silly. Makes just as much sense as climbing a rocky cliff, if you ask me.

Normally it was required to wear a helmet. Mike assured me he didn't need it, nor did he want climbing shoes. He wore, instead, his brand-new hiking boots clearly purchased for the trip—monstrous leather things that looked like they'd been made in the Alps by gnomes.

I tied the rope to his harness and stepped back, pulling in slack and readying myself to belay. A crowd of kids had gathered, and other parents. He was the last to climb that day, so folks sat around to watch. The pressure was on, but, as a thespian, Mike was ready for the challenge. It may have been my imagination, but I'm pretty sure he may have posed a moment, like models do at the end of the runway. He began to climb.

At first it seemed to go okay. But the thing is, those weird little ballet slipper shoes that climbers wear, with the sticky rubber soles? They *really* help. Comfortable they are not, but they've been designed with the input of climbers for decades. Mike was powering his way up the rock, using all muscle and mostly arms. It's a ton easier to find good footholds and slowly make your way up; your legs can comfortably carry your weight a whole lot better than your arms.

I could see Mike was sweating. He reached a part of the climb I'd been calling "the crux" all day. About fifteen feet up, it was the intersection of two natural lines in the rock made of cracks and little ledges. Because these lines converged, climbers had to essentially hug the rock, using the flats of their hands to maintain contact, and mincingly step their feet up a few moves before another reasonable handhold presented itself. It was a bit scary because climbers just had to trust that their feet would hold them, and try to generate friction with their outspread hands against the rock to maintain position. While kids sometimes don't have the reach or muscle adults do, most had been able to navigate this section because their strength-to-weight ratio favored the moves required. A guy like Mike would have to really mantle—use a downward-facing palm on the rock to push up—on an almost nonexistent bulge in the rock to keep moving upward.

One of the fun aspects of rock climbing is the repartee between climber and belayer. Often the position of the belayer offers a visual perspective that allows them to see holds in the rock that the climber can't see. It can either help climbers or send them into hysteria.

"By your right knee, a little knob!"

"Here?" asks the climber, pawing wildly with their foot.

"Yeah, wait. Reach your left arm up, shove your third finger up to the second knuckle into that tiny crack as big as Helen Mirren's crow's feet while mantling with your other hand down by your ankle, then smear your left foot on that slab. No, the practically nonexistent one!"

It's usually at this point, trembling and awash with sweat, that the climber gives up and falls back to be lowered down—dignity shattered— like a sack of broken dreams.

"Go Dad!" yelled Toph. Everyone was watching, yelling random snippets of encouragement and advice. Voices echoed off the rocks as Mike stalled, unsure how to proceed past the crux.

That's when Elvis leg set in.

For the uninitiated: Elvis leg is a condition where the stress and strain of climbing cause your leg to shake uncontrollably, most noticeable in novice climbers. I suffered from a debilitating case of Elvis leg the first dozen times I went climbing. I'd be so tight and tense that a few minutes into any climb my legs were shaking like crazy, adrenaline and lactic acid pouring through my bloodstream. My legs would cramp and bounce so much you could practically hear echoes of "You Ain't Nothin' but a Hound Dog."

Probably the worst part of Elvis leg is the fact that it can't be controlled. Like shivering in the cold, it's involuntary.

Mike's leg was shaking like crazy. He was precariously clinging to the rock.

"Tension!" he said.

Usually, climbers yell something like "tension" or "falling" when they think they're going to lose their grip and fall. It's a warning to the belayer to brake the rope and be ready for a fall.

But Mike had other plans. He snaked a hand up the rope and hauled himself up. He did so surreptitiously—sort of holding the rope in between his body and the rock where it was hard to see by those of us on the ground.

"Got it," he said.

The deal with top roping, generally, is that the rope is there for safety in case you fall. Obviously, you *could* just pull yourself up and along the rope to reach the top. But that would defeat the purpose, the whole challenge of the thing. With kids, I wouldn't let them do it; they could always try again to surmount the challenge. I felt a little awkward; maybe Mike didn't understand? But there was no way; he'd been hearing me all day exhort kids to not grab the rope.

"Tension!"

His big alpine boots were smashing against the rock, and again I felt his weight pull the rope. I hauled in slack reflexively, and he used the tight rope to pull himself up again. He was huffing and puffing now, trying to speed up the rock.

"Hey Mike," I began.

"Tension!"

He was powering up, using the rope to haul himself up as quickly as possible. I was pulling in slack fast, his weight against the rope as he used it to lug himself upward. He hit the top of the route, touched the carabiner at the top (I had kids do it to signify that they'd completed that route), and leaned back into his harness. He pumped a fist into the air.

"Yeah, Dad!" Toph yelled. Kids and adults clapped and yelled congratulations. I was a bit abashed for him. Um, did anyone notice that I was basically hauling him up on the rope? I lowered him to the ground. Toph ran over and they high-fived each other. Toph's eyes were bright. "Dad, you nailed it!" he said, practically dancing with pride. I could see the sweat pouring down Mike's face and neck.

Mike came up to me, hand held up palm outward for a high five. I gave him one.

There is something admirable about the unabashed self-regard he possessed. The way he moved through the world so sure of himself. It felt so alien to me, since I made choices with knee-jerk reflexiveness and then castigated myself for being so impulsive.

Individuals similar in temperament, solipsistic and shallow, abound in popular imagination. Nineteenth-century novels, in particular, often sketch these flaky, self-absorbed characters with relish, depicting them as mildly neurotic women (usually) sitting in drawing rooms nattering endlessly about marriage prospects, dresses, money, balls and soirees. A portrait of an aristocracy so bound up in its own importance that a kind of silly senescence and impotence have galvanized.

Now we have the entertainment machine of Hollywood offering portraits of self-absorption. Movies and TV have created an entire pantheon of male slobs who are endlessly absorbed in the pursuit of their own hedonistic ends, yet do so raffishly and with aw-shucks self-deprecation. The Seth Rogens, Adam Sandlers, and Will Ferrells of the world depict this same character in dozens of films—the man-child with the heart of gold. We see him in movie after movie. A grown man in a baggy T-shirt eschewing responsibility in favor of beer-chugging slackerdom. It is an archetype I'm personally familiar with.

The popularity of this phenotype may lie in the propensity for men to forgive themselves for their worst tendencies—chalk up bad behavior to a kind of slovenly charming, laissez-faire attitude. But I can't help wondering if it's just a narrow slice of white privilege. After all, the white men-children depicted in films like *Knocked Up*, *Step Brothers*, *Old School*, and *Billy Madison* are allowed to be slobs; our culture gives permission to white people to be shaggy ne'er-do-wells as long as there is a streak of beneficence in there somewhere. Rarely is there a Black character who gets to be the stoner, the semi-employed slacker, unless it's in films like the *Friday* franchise helmed by Ice Cube, in which case most of the humor is an intraspecific back and forth of stereotypes within the Black community. Arguably, the most masterful effort to toss this paradigmatic forgiveness for the white male oaf on its head is the brilliant *Harold and Kumar Go to White Castle*, depicting an Asian and Indian weed-smoking duo with an epic case of the munchies. The movie does more to explain race in America than most.

The self-concerned white dude gets labeled as charmingly louche, behavior excused, and the culture at large is complicit in making women adhere to wildly unreal standards of feminine beauty while guys get to drain Budweiser, gobble plates of wings, and have their Dad bods called sexy. Watching Mike high-five his way back to camp, I couldn't help but think of the way we excuse men for almost everything, an aspect of culture I've benefited from time and again.

That night, after we'd gotten the kids to sleep, the adults sat around as the stars of J Tree spun above us. As we chatted and watched the stars come out, my feelings about Mike softened. Maybe he was as lost as anyone. After all, it couldn't be easy to head out, every day, to casting calls and get told you're too old, too young, too something. Perhaps he'd built up his bravado as a kind of armor against the constant failure of not getting parts. As we sat under a canopy of a billion stars, Mike told us how, when he'd been a male model in his youth, he'd been in France for a fashion show. He and a friend had decided to go ski the Alps. They had no winter clothing, so went instead in their model-wear, $500 jeans and designer sweaters. Mike told us how they rented skis and spent the day carving the slopes wearing their street clothes. I loved that image—despite his narcissism, there was something so irreverently charming about two chiseled models bombing down the frozen Alps, dressed in haute couture, looking good and going fast.

14

Pink Volcano of the Mojave

ROAD TRIPS RUN THE RISK OF EITHER DEADENING THE SENSES WITH hours of monotonous sameness rushing by the window at sixty miles per hour, reminding us that no matter how fast or where we go we're still mired in our own inescapable neurosis, or they loosen the spirit from the anchor of the daily grind and lift us up on the breeze to soar, like our hands sticking out the window planing on the wind. But however they make us feel, there are never enough places to stop and pee.

I pulled the car over into the parking lot. The blazing sun baked every square inch of ground, and I could feel my hair practically cooking as I walked out toward the crater. The middle schoolers I was taking on this adventure—Death Valley, Joshua Tree, Red Rock Canyon—ran past me shrieking toward the rim. Ubehebe Crater is one of the more distinctive landmarks in Death Valley—an area already stuffed with more landmarks than Disneyworld. A massive half-mile-wide pit in the middle of a desolate landscape, the crater is the collapsed cone of a volcano. Visiting Ubehebe is a strange experience. To saunter down the black, sandy volcanic sands into the baking calm of the center is to enter another world. The Timbisha Shoshone believe their people came from Ubehebe Crater. The story goes that Coyote was carrying the Timbisha Shoshone in a basket across the desert and set the basket down to sleep. As Coyote napped, the people snuck out of the basket and dispersed across the desert. The crater is now all that's left, a depression of a giant basket.

Creation myths such as these always make more sense to me than biblical tales. Like many Indigenous peoples, the Shoshone's stories about themselves are rooted in place, defined in part by the landscape around them. I always find these narratives compelling. Hardly surprising; bookshelves are full of white dudes like me trying to force our way into some comprehension of the natural world using native mythology as a guide. We're like the weirdo unpopular kids in middle school trying to hang out with the cool, popular crowd so that we can be associated with something sublime rather than recognized for our awkwardness and body odor.

We all climbed down the sides of the crater, where the heat pressed down on us in stifling stillness. The rocky, wrinkled walls were reddish brown, and black sand had poured down over eons in great huge fans along the bottom. I had brought a book of Native American origin stories to read to the students at night, but wondered if I even should. What was I trying to do, after all, bringing them here, to this place, junked up on McDonald's and Subway, for a glimpse at a landscape that is so deeply steeped in Indigenous memory, only to roar off again in our minivans to some other sacred spot.

In *The Songlines*, Bruce Chatwin travels to the outback of Australia trying to learn about the "Dreamtime" of the Aborigines. The book—published in 1987—was a critical success, cementing Chatwin's reputation as a brilliant travel writer. Dreamtime is a complex idea, a difficult topic for a westerner like me to conjure into words. It's a series of foundational myths about the creation of the world by ancient spirits, so it happened a long time ago and yet is a living, breathing philosophy and internal compass. See? Dreamtime, if nothing else, escapes the boxy confines of Western labels and thought. Part of Dreamtime (to be really clear, these ideas can't be expressed with clarity by someone like me; I don't know if any non-Aboriginal could understand) are the "Songlines." Both stories and maps, Songlines seem to be central to the Dreamtime and the way Aboriginal people navigate both their internal and external realities. But even that description doesn't do it justice; the Songlines contain their mythology and beliefs as well. They are a collective personification bound up in rhythm and cadence. One aspect of the Songlines is that an Aboriginal traveler could "sing" their way across the landscape, noting geographical features (two emus sleeping, for example, denoting emu-esque-looking rock outcroppings) as they moved, the song and country around them blending into a kind of spiritual map. Chatwin bounces around the outback in this book, meeting Aborigines and trying to come to some understanding of the nature of walking and Indigenous wisdom and travel, among other subjects.

It's yet another travel book written by a white man using native ideologies as a springboard for personal exploration, a kind of passive literary colonization. I can't really blame Chatwin though. First, the idea of Aboriginal Dreamtime and Songlines is so deeply fascinating it's hard not to get obsessed. Secondly, Chatwin's book is brilliant. As a writer he's marvelous. As a privileged white male writer myself, I sympathize with Chatwin's need to associate with Indigenous wisdom, as cringe-worthy as that kind of bookish appropriation can be. It's clear that as a certain type of white male writer, we're aware that we've *lost something*. That by virtue of issuing forth from the momentous propulsion of Western thought, we've corralled and domesticated our own imaginations. We—I—seek out any identification with Indigenous ideas because I know my own thought patterns are so patterned by the hierarchies of Western intellectualization that I'm removed from a real firsthand understanding. I'm distanced from direct experience of the world around me by objective rationale and classification. This whole thing smacks of the romantic notion of "the noble savage," I know. But just because my longings are cliché and thoroughly debunked doesn't mean I feel them any less intensely.

Books like Chatwin's are like explorations into wild landscapes. They are the manifestation of longing—an individual hurls themself into the unknown to find, what? Themself, maybe? Meaning? It is the kind of journey I daydream intensely about, usually while sitting in my car outside Chipotle waiting for my order, or listening to the Muzak echo tinnily from my phone as I wait on hold with Verizon because I was overcharged on this month's bill, and thinking, *Well, this sucks. There's gotta be something else.*

Chatwin travels to Australia and co-opts the mystery of the Aborigines for his own artistic ends; a yearning for communion with some realer version of himself, perhaps. An understanding of some core aspect of identity bound up in movement, in being nomadic. If I'm being honest, I'm no different. I've spent a good portion of my life nosing around the world's woodsy corners. I think I go to these places in the hope that seeking will strip away the layers of whiteness, civilization, and good sense. Power wash the layers of domestication armoring my heart and mind with a good dose of the outdoors, and maybe I'll glimpse some version of my authentic self. That, perhaps, by tracing these ancient tracks of Indigenous wisdom, I can be in communion with a more concrete version of myself. Because, for some of us, two-car garages and frequent flier miles are not enough. Or maybe too much?

But with a writer like Chatwin, or any traveler who heads out into places like the Mojave Desert, there is, obviously, a risk of romanticizing and exoticising the "other." Collecting stories that don't belong to you to place in your curio cabinet and show off to your friends. It's also possible to make mysterious things that are, in fact, mundane—to imbue Indigenous ideas with an aura of magic they don't contain. I listened to a conversation between Black artists once, and one of them said that he was sick and tired of using art to proclaim "Black excellence." He said that what he wanted was for some twenty-year-old Black kid to be able to get stoned and play Xbox all day. That real equity will be achieved when people of color can be just as unapologetically mediocre as white people. It made me think of the way some white writers, especially, can approach Indigenous culture. Maybe the "other" isn't different. Maybe I'm just looking at things the wrong way, hiking trails and scouring deserts looking for some secret that doesn't exist.

What a white writer does by extracting Indigenous stories like ore from the earth is take away the agency of first peoples to contain their own legacy. You can't blame us, though. If forced to tell only our own stories, books would be full of nothing but tales of how bilious Lord Abercrombie got all gouty and farted into his breeches whilst wiping aristocratic boogers on his waistcoat.

It can sometimes feel like we've lost something. As though once you've boiled down the white, privileged existence, all you're left with are Franzen-esque screeds about how our mothers didn't love us enough and how our ambition to write the great American novel was torpedoed by the need to get a job. Boo-hoo. It's no wonder white men start so many wars. We need *something* to write about.

The kids explored and yelled, complained of being thirsty and having sand in their shoes, and eventually we all got back in the cars and trundled off to the next spot we wanted to visit. The landscape of the Mojave sped by: ochres and browns, reds, and about one hundred shades of beige. The shining white of salt pan flats, the flinty grays of the mountains ringing the valleys. It was Martian and weird and undeniably beautiful, but as I headed south through the desert I began to understand how much my own use and enjoyment of these lands was a form of theft. How my love of the outdoors—my attraction to wild places—was a form of colonization, sort of an imperialist strategy outfitted by Patagonia and North Face.

Of course, the strains of appropriation run through my whole life. I grew up on the banks of the Neshobe River in Vermont, a name with opaque origins. Possibly an Algonquin word brought north to Vermont by early white settlers, the word is first seen in Littleton, Massachusetts, in the mid-eighteenth century, and means "double water," or perhaps the space between two bodies of water. In any case, a land speculator named Josiah Powers headed up to what was then the New Hampshire land grants and brought the name with him. It was applied to the town in the central mountains of Vermont where I grew up. It was soon replaced by the name "Brandon," but the little stream that ran through the town kept the name, as did the elementary school I attended.

My favorite movie as a kid was *Windwalker*. A rarity, in that it was a film about Native Americans without reference to white settlers. Based on a novel by Blaine M. Yorgason, it tells the story of a Cheyenne chief's untimely death, resurrection, and battle with the rival Crow people. An attempt at authenticity was made—the languages of the Cheyenne and Crow are used with English subtitles—but the main roles were played by white actors. In a cruel bit of irony, the corny trailer I looked up on YouTube describes it as "the most authentic Indian film ever made." Yet it stars a Brit and a Yank.

The book I read and reread growing up was *Call of the Wild* by Jack London, wherein the hero, the dog Buck, enacts the penultimate scene by murdering the Yeehat Indian tribe in revenge for killing his white master, John Thorton. It is not mentioned that Thorton is, of course, trespassing on Yeehat lands, or that Thorton is part of a wave of white settlers rapaciously searching for gold in the rivers of the Yukon Territory. But that book and its messages are so deeply burned in my brain that it became part of how I saw the outdoors, adventures, and myself.

Because of books like London's and a desire for outdoor adventure, I'd eventually end up with Outward Bound. Early adventures in Florida took me down rivers in central Florida, the last stronghold of the Seminole, who fought a bitter war against white settlers for decades. Later, I'd hike the Sierra Nevada. The section of the range in northern California was the home of Ishi, whose life story is perhaps the saddest, and most emblematic. Considered to be one of the only members left of his tribe—though specialists would later connect him with various "umbrella" tribes of the region—Ishi was captured near Mount Lassen in northern California. He was poked and prodded and studied at the University of Berkeley, and they gave him a job. Janitor. He eventually died of tuberculosis. Most of his family had been killed in the Three Knolls Massacre of 1865, in which around forty Yahi were murdered. Ishi's people were attacked while they were sleeping.

It goes on and on. While living in Los Angeles I explored the San Gabriel Mountains almost daily, peaks named in conjunction with local Christian missions that decimated the culture of the Gabrielino-Tongva, people who had lived in the San Gabriel valley prior to white settlers moving into the area. Even now, I teach at Champlain College, named after a French explorer who led the way for colonization of lands previously occupied by the Abenaki, Huron, and Algonquin peoples.

My love of the outdoors rests on a legacy of usurpation, theft, and genocide.

I married a woman descended from the Indigenous peoples of the Sonoran Desert. After decades of blithely tramping across native lands, obliviously singing the praises of white conservationists who sought to protect these "unpeopled" lands (because they'd already disposed of the Indians living there through the judicious distribution of blankets à la smallpox and a healthy dollop of genocidal Manifest Destiny), I've come to wonder about my marriage. Did I find my wife attractive because she had thick, straight black hair, brown skin, and dark eyes? Yes. Was I bowled over by what I saw as her exotic looks? Again, yes. Does that mean I've "tokenized" her? Seen her race as "other," thus unknowable and mysterious and compellingly alien? Yes. Do I still find her smoking hot because of her Indigenous good looks? Yes. Is that racist? Probably. Guilty as charged.

We pulled off the highway at one of those ubiquitous, neon-lit truck stops somewhere in the area of the Nevada/California state line, heading into the Nevada desert to visit some old historic mines on the way south to Joshua Tree. It was dinnertime, and the kids piled out of the van and into fast-food joints to fill their bellies with Brazilian rainforest beef and cloned fries.

The kids purchased their grub and slammed and flopped to the cheer-less, plasticky tables to eat.

I watched one of the kids, David, cruise through his burger. It was impressive, the speed at which he ate. Fries and then shake were finished in record time. He must've had the metabolism of a field mouse, because David headed back up to the counter and bought another strawberry shake. He gamely began slurping down his second shake, his intake at this point surpassing thirty ounces of plasticine milkshake that looked like melted Barbies.

As we left the restaurant, some of the boys started grab-assing. Punch-ing each other, grabbing friends, headlocks, shin kicks, farts, belches. Class acts. David was involved in the fun. He was practically vibrating, wound up on boy-energy and about sixteen thousand calories of milkshake. He'd probably consumed a bushel of sugarcane. The kids were whirling about under the hot, windy evening sky of the Mojave.

It was at this point that a jitterbugging David, who was now overfed, overstimulated, and overwhelmed, projectile-vomited.

It was a fantastic pink arc. I don't believe I've ever seen anything quite so awe-inspiring. It was like the fountains of the Bellagio in Vegas were erupting from David's mouth. *There was just so much of it*, and it kept com-ing in one long, continuous stream. David's digestive system maintained the pressure of a fairly large bore garden hose for a couple of seconds. It was like firemen were using Pepto Bismol to put out a blaze.

Maybe I would never understand what was really going on in the stories of the Aborigines or Shoshone. I could know it, but not really *know* it. But I knew then, crisscrossing that landscape, and in the years since, visiting and exploring wild places, that traversing the landscape is a form of storytelling. That, for me, I can make meaning—of myself, of the places I visit, of the choices I've made—by moving through mountains and forests. I was a visitor to these lands; that I knew. The Indigenous people who were here before had a connection to this place I'd probably never truly grasp. But, like them, I needed these mountains and trails to find my way through life.

Their stories told of the origins of their people, the creation of their world. I looked at David. What could my own legacy provide? As a white

European American, my story was one of colonial conquest, Manifest Destiny served with a side of eugenics. Kids were now screaming and running away from David as though he'd just tossed down some plutonium in a pile in front of him.

The Shoshone. Abenaki. Huron and Seminole. Their stories aren't mine, I thought. But I will have my own. Someday, I will tell the story of the Pink Volcano of the Mojave.

15

The British Explosion

*The thing you have always suspected about yourself the minute you
become a tourist is true: a tourist is an ugly human being.*
                    —JAMAICA KINCAID, FROM *A SMALL PLACE*

AFTER MY ADVENTURES WITH OUTWARD BOUND I WANDERED WEST TO
Southern California, where I briefly flirted with going to an exorbitantly
expensive college but dropped out after a year, deciding that while getting
massively stoned in dorm rooms and listening to Dinosaur Jr was fun and
all, there were other avenues I wanted to explore. Leveraging my minimal
outdoor skills and experience working with youth at risk in Florida, I got
a job at a small private school in Los Angeles.

I've never traveled much. In my twenties—when most young folks
satisfy their wanderlust by backpacking around Eastern Europe or Southeast Asia—I was busy trying to consume every beer and Jägermeister
shot in Los Angeles, which left me little time for international escapades.
Despite this lack of experience, I was chosen to help chaperone a middle school trip through Europe. My qualifications were a) I was male,
thus balanced the gender equation as the teacher orchestrating the trip
was *Ms.* Demott; and b) I had never murdered a middle schooler in cold
blood. This second qualification is no small feat, as anyone who has spent
more than an hour in a room full of twelve-year-old hormonal preteens
can attest to.

I knew next to nothing about Europe. The itinerary was scheduled at
an astonishing clip: We were to land in London and spend about twenty
hours there, then be whisked south on a whirlwind tour of France, see
Switzerland out the windows of a train, and finish in Italy with visits
to Florence, Pisa, and Rome. All in seven days. The Grand Tour in a
microdose.

I had been to France twice before, once as part of a high school French
class I was in. My path to French V was paved with a level of astounding
linguistic mediocrity. I could never, even if my life depended on it, speak
in any tense other than pidgin present. My accent made me sound like I'd

swallowed my toothbrush sideways and was trying to cough it back up while asking directions to the Metro. I couldn't conjugate the third person plural of verbs, thus spoke to everyone in first person plural, "we" or "us," a language shortcut that had me asking complete strangers questions like "Where can we go to the bathroom?" which sounded like an invitation it most certainly was not.

Astride in Paris, our rowdy group of American high schoolers craned our necks at the city around us. This was Paris, the most romantic city in the world, or so we were told. Nexus of European cosmopolitanism, center of intellectual enlightenment. If the world is your oyster, then Paris is the pearl. The city was laid out in all its glory before us, a million adventures to be had.

We immediately went to the nearest little shop next to our hotel, bought armfuls of beer and packs of smokes, and sat in our tiny rooms, drinking beer and smugly congratulating ourselves on our worldliness. One of the lessons I've learned from travel is that when you visit some far-flung place populated with provincial rustics, they seem quaint. When you travel and you *are* a provincial rustic, you look like an idiot.

Chaperoning the middle schoolers would be my third trip to the European continent. Besides the high school French trip, I'd gone to Paris when I was about five or six. My grandparents took our family on a barge trip down the canals of France. We slept, cooked, and traveled on a converted barge that visited little towns and villages. My memory of the barge is mostly taken up by a set of small metal Napoleonic soldiers I played with a great deal, mostly because that was the only toy on the boat. The barge was tight yet cozy, and I remember being quite content to line up Napoleon's army in rank and file and then smash them with my grubby little fists.

One day during the trip the whole family rode bikes to visit the countryside. Vineyards and wine-tasting figured prominently in the day's activities, and the adults grew progressively more cheerful and expansive about the wines they drank. I had not yet learned to ride a bike, so I had to sit, precariously perched, on my Aunt Ann's handlebars. This was in the late 1970s, so helmets and general safety measures had yet to be invented. There had been a light drizzle all day. As our family zigzagged down the road, veins flowing with *bonhomie* and cabernet, we came to a long hill sloping down to the canal where the barge was docked. My aunt had been informed about how the rubber brakes on our dilapidated French bikes wouldn't work at optimum levels in the rain, the principle of friction upon which they relied being subverted by water. The collective wisdom was that it was best to walk the bikes down the hill.

Aunt Ann pooh-poohed this notion (I think she may have actually said "pooh-pooh") and invited me to saddle up on her handlebars and join her in a downhill ride back to the barge.

I gamely clambered aboard. Looking back, it's a classic indication of an underdeveloped cerebral cortex.

She pushed off and we began coasting downhill, the wet pavement zizzing underneath us, a fine spray of water rooster-tailing off our tires. Tiny water droplets speckled my face. It felt good. All the adults had told us not to do it, and we were doing it anyway. To go against grown-up remonstration as a child? Manna from heaven.

As our speed increased, my aunt clenched the rusted old hand-brake levers. The prognostications of the rest of the family proved prophetic: The brakes simply emitted a squeal like a Gallic pig being goosed with a pool cue but did little to slow our bombardier's dive.

Moments like this tell us who we really are. The bike rocketed downhill, and there was clearly no stopping it by conventional methods. The road ran diagonally down the face of the hill. To our right it dropped off steeply, to our left was a bank of scree and weeds. My aunt came to the harsh but necessary conclusion that the only hope of checking our rapid descent was through the application of rudimentary physics. As we shot down the hill, wind whipping back the hair from our faces, water stinging our eyes, she veered the bike into the bank. Because I was sitting on the handlebars, legs dangling, I was like a fleshy hood ornament when the bike suddenly arrested forward motion. I was catapulted into the prickers and gravel, slamming hard and tumbling to a stop.

There is something about being slightly drunk on a bike that envelopes the rider in a mist of assumed invulnerability. Perhaps it's the *joie de vivre*, or the looseness of the joints. Either way, Aunt Ann was more or less okay, as was I, minor cuts and bruises notwithstanding. Shaken, but more or less whole. We'd narrowly avoided a decent maiming.

Aunt Ann was not through, however. She was not about to let near disaster deter her from being contrary, a disorder I believe I inherited. She picked herself up, righted the bike, and asked me if I wanted to try again. I got back on the handlebars, which tells you something about my decision-making capabilities. We careened down the hill once more, spectacularly crashing again at the bottom. *Tant pis.*

My experience of Europe, therefore, was bound up in those memories—a young boy subject to the whims of adults, and a teenager so wrapped up in self-consciousness he couldn't see the forest for *les arbres.* I was relieved, then, years later as a chaperone on the middle school trip, when we arrived on the continent, to see that as part of our tour we'd be riding on one of those big, gaudy buses you see careening around the world near popular tourist destinations. And this may make me sound tacky, but there is something to be said for traveling through Europe on a big coach bus. Like many Americans, I was happy to have Europe prepackaged and served to me like a convenience store snack.

The tour was a blur of English and French tourist locales and jet lag. As part of the package, we had a tour guide named Brian, an affable Brit whose snaggle-toothed smile and thick accent charmed all of us. He seemed utterly at home in the world regardless of where we went, happily chatting in French at the restaurants where we ate lukewarm ratatouille and Ms. Demott and I snuck glasses of wine at lunch.

Eventually, after days of speed-tourism, our massive tour bus rolled into Rome. Obviously, I am not the only one who has walked through Rome until my feet ached, transfixed by visible layers of history. Seeing the Coliseum in the gloom of the evening is such a fixture in the zeitgeist imaginings of archaeological history that to say anything about the experience practically demands cliché. But it was pretty cool, and I felt—as just about everyone has before me—the stretch of history all around me, the weight of time in that place.

The kids wanted to hit the city. They wanted excitement, they wanted danger. They didn't want to simply sit in the lobby of the shabby hotel we were staying in playing cards. They cajoled and pleaded and begged, and finally Brian admitted that, yes, there was a dance club nearby that allowed teenagers. The kids riotously cheered, hormones flooding their bloodstreams at the thought of shaking their groove thang at a European discotheque. Brian led us out, and we walked through the darkening streets of Rome, passing little cafes and narrow streets and the odd Parthenon.

The discotheque was a subterranean room, black walled and strobed with flashes of light and some of the worst music I've ever heard. It wasn't particularly busy at that hour, but the place was maybe a third full. The kids immediately began buying Cokes and heading out to the dance floor to twirl and shake and twist about. Ms. Demott and I positioned ourselves away from the dance floor against the wall, smiling grimly as the kids shrieked and bobbed to the pounding sounds of Europe's latest pop hits. Then Brian wandered by, and the students—who by this point had fallen in love with his sarcastic English wit—rushed him and dragged him out onto the floor. I thought he'd demur, as we were, offering a *no, no, no thank you. I don't dance.* But I was wrong.

He hit the dance floor with the confidence of a matador. As he neared the knot of American middle schoolers amid the Euro masses, his step became a jerky, robotic duck waddle. Dances with names like the jitterbug, the Spongebob, and the Dougie exist. This one, if it had a name, would be called The British Explosion. Syncopated, sharp arm movements—with index fingers pointing like guns—were incongruous with a rapid, campfire-extinguishing step I immediately nicknamed "the logger stomp" in my head. There was a vibrating quality to Brian, a kind of full-body seizure. He was somehow able to simultaneously stick out his tongue and bite his lip with the classic white man's overbite. I don't know how he did it. It was as though he'd just emerged from deep in the wilderness and had never before seen other humans or heard music, and was tapping into some primal, ecstatic spirit that caused his body to convulse and shake. His movements seemed closer to a medical condition than a dance. It was the sort of awful dancing that makes the viewer feel embarrassed for the dancer.

And yet, he *owned* it, with such absolute confidence and joy. The kids screamed and clapped, their eyes shining bright and mouths wide open in the happiest leering grins I've ever seen. They howled and cheered, and Brian just went at it harder, committing himself mind, body, and soul to the most horrific dancing I've ever seen.

Walking back to the hotel late that night, the kids talking way too loudly as we made our way through the streets of Rome, I thought about The Spectacle of Brian. I thought about how Ms. Demott and I, pillars of respectability that we were, had just sat off to the side. I looked at the shining faces of the kids, the way they shoved and jostled and pushed each other as we wandered back to the hotel, their faces sweaty and flushed and happy.

After about an hour of shushing and shooing, we got the kids into their rooms. Ms. Demott headed off to bed, and I wandered back down to the deserted lobby. I stared out the window, and realized that I felt bad for not dancing. When would I ever be in Rome again? Or Europe for that matter? I'd chosen decorum over fun, boringly staid New England stolidness over exuberance and joy.

I headed back out into the streets and wandered around. Eventually, I found a little nightclub. Upstairs was a small cafe, and I ordered a beer from the zinc-topped bar. *Birra*, I said, brutally botching the accent. The bartender sighed and put down a bottle of Peroni. I went down to the cavernous gloom of the dance floor, located beneath the ground floor in a kind of bunker. It was much smaller than the one we'd visited previously, and practically empty.

I am not a good dancer. But I stepped out onto the floor, left my dignity back along the wall in the shadows, pointed my fingers, and shook my moneymaker. Because there are two types of people in this world: those that dance, and those that wish they had.

16

Bear Baggin'

THE KIDS GROANED AND WHINED ALL THE WAY UP OVER KEARSARGE Pass in the southern Sierras of California. Just south of Mount Whitney, the tallest peak in the Lower 48, Kearsarge Pass, at 11,760 feet, was a favorite trip during the years I taught in California. On this particular trek Aaron and I were shepherding a group of kids into the Rae Lakes region, a beautiful area within the Sierras. High alpine lakes, rocky jutting peaks, summer snowfields, and marmots—the place had it all. It was like walking into an Ansel Adams photograph. On this particular jaunt, we had planned to be out for six days. Nothing epic, but for an Angeleno kid, or any city-dweller, six days in a tent is a long time.

Aaron Kenny was a husky guy in his early twenties. He wore a trucker hat that read "Damn Seagulls" across the front, replete with a white painted splotch on the bill. He was abstemious—said he'd spent his teenage years coming home from school, shoving two bottles of Corona from his parents' fridge into the pockets of his jeans, heading up to his bedroom, and using the beers to wash down Adderall and Ritalin. He'd sobered up but lived a Bukowski lifestyle in Eagle Rock—a suburb of Los Angeles—that is, if Bukowski was a teetotaling vegan. He told me once how fruit leather snacks could be substituted for toothbrushing on hasty mornings, information I found both gross and potentially practical.

We got settled into our campsite by the river, and Aaron and I led the kids out in pairs to various spots in a wide semicircle around the basecamp. On this particular trip, the students were instructed to build a homemade shelter for themselves. It was early afternoon, a beautiful spring day, and the kids got to work building their shelters. It was always interesting to me to see how kids would respond to this particular challenge. They were given a big blue tarp and a coil of parachute cord. That was it. They would build little stone-walled huts, brush piles with chambers dug out of the center, lean-tos, and, one time, what resembled a tiki hut. Kids have an interesting perspective on the line that divides the practical from the aesthetic.

I could tell Aaron was a bit unnerved by being so far out in the mountains. Though we were only a single, solid day's hike in, it was enough to surprise him with the totality of the silence, the complete absence of civilization. He had the desperate look of a Hollywood starlet who's out of Botox.

I'm no Thoreau. While I love being outside and in the wilderness, it doesn't feel necessarily transcendent. However, I do feel *at ease* in the backcountry. I love being away from the pressures of schedules, domestic responsibilities, jobs, appointments, demands, and all the addictive pleasures of convenience: streaming TV, microwaved corn dogs, Costco. To have your sphere reduced to a hissing camp stove with a pot of water just beginning to steam to make hot chocolate on a chill morning is a way to ground myself. It is as though, stripped of the hum of the world, I get the chance to return to myself for a visit. My days in civilization consist of a lot of activity, but it's an open question whether or not any of it is fulfilling in any substantial way. But dry socks after a wet trekking day? The best feeling ever.

Aaron and I made it back into camp after spreading the kids out throughout the forest as the sky began to gray and darken with night. We pulled on our headlamps and prepared to hang our food in a tree to keep it away from bears. Normally, the best thing to do is bring a bear-barrel, a heavy-duty plastic container that fits snugly in the bottom of a backpack. The girth and shape have been designed so that bears can't get a grip on the plastic. They end up batting it around but can't get in. I hadn't invested in them—they were cost prohibitive to my meager supply budget, which barely covered food and gas to get us to the mountains—and chose instead to hang what was commonly called a "bear bag." Basically, I'd load all the food into a backpack, then find a tree with a branch that stuck out horizontally at least twenty feet from the ground. I'd toss some cord over the branch and hoist up the bag. The idea was that a bear couldn't reach it from the ground, and couldn't get out on the limb to hoist up the bag due to a lack of opposable thumbs.

It was dark by the time we got all the food packed away. We had also collected anything else the bears might like—deodorant, which the kids weren't even supposed to bring but many did anyway, toothpaste, sunscreen, and anything else vaguely scented and food-like.

Aaron and I headed out beyond the camp to find a good tree. I was usually pretty assiduous about hanging food in a way that ensured it wouldn't be eaten by bears. I solidly recognized the danger of bringing black bears near camp. Though not as dangerous as a grizzly, they're still bears. Bears will be bears, after all.

Aaron's orbit of me was growing tighter and tighter as it got darker and darker. It was becoming apparent to me, as night fell and I could see more and more of the whites of his eyes in my headlamp's glow, that he was a little afraid of the dark. Most people are. If held at gunpoint, I'd have to admit that I, too, get the heebie-jeebies out in the woods at night. There must be some elemental evolutionary switch that gets thrown as the sun goes down, where our perspective goes from that of predator to prey, because the second I start walking through the dark woods the hair on my neck stands up, my scrotum tightens, and I start walking briskly like I had a double helping of All Bran for breakfast and am headed to the bathroom.

I found a suitable tree, got a rope over a branch, and hoisted up the backpack, tying off the line high on the tree. The large pack filled with all our food swung lightly back and forth. The darkness was complete now.

"Have you ever faced down a bear before?" Aaron asked me, in what I thought a rather endearing, earnest, and twelve-year-oldish sort of way.

"Yeah, I have," I chuckled, gearing up to launch into one of my many stories that had been proven by the FDA to be an effective sleep aid. We swung our headlamps back toward camp and turned away from the hanging food bag. Aaron was crowding me in the dark, our shoulders brushing. I began to tell my story as we headed back toward where we'd set up our tents earlier.

"*Fwooomp!*"

From behind us, I heard the food bag hit the ground. Aaron and I looked at each other, blinding each other with the LED glare of our headlamps for a moment. I turned to see a bear next to our food bag. Caught in the spotlight of my headlamp, its eyes reflected as yellow disks.

Aaron screamed. I stood frozen, blood pumping through my body as I felt my brain go instantly offline, replaced by a white scrim of sheer panic. The bear grabbed the pack in its teeth—*in its teeth*, people—and with a burst of incredible speed, galloped off into the darkness. I heard it splash heavily across a stream behind our camp.

"Fucking bear!" Aaron yelled, his voice sounding like his testicles were in the bear's jaws instead of our food bag. I turned, but Aaron was already sprinting wildly back toward camp. I turned back to where the bear had disappeared into the brush. My first thought was that I should give chase. My second thought was that that was never, ever going to happen.

As my sphincter slowly uncoiled and rational thought returned, I tried to think of what to do. How would we get our food back? Should I track the bear? That would only work, I realized, if I knew anything whatsoever about tracking, which I don't. As I stood, immobilized by my own instinctive fear, a realization dawned on me with a jolt. All the kids were spread out through a wide arc of forest, and there was a brave, hungry, and apparently rather pushy bear in the area.

Black bears aren't normally aggressive. But they can be, when the pickings are good and they are hungry. A bear that was willing to play tug o' war with a backpack full of food would be willing to sniff out a hidden candy bar or bag of Skittles. I could picture some of the middle schoolers I'd brought, happily munching a bag of illicit M&Ms and looking up to find a bear shouldering its way into their shelter, jaws open and slavering. It was not a positive image from a PR standpoint.

Aaron was petrified. He dove into his tent, and his voice was shaky and high pitched. When I grasped the zipper to open the fly and talk to him, he uttered a sharp squeak. I shone my light into the tent, and his hip, urban, plastic-framed writerly specs couldn't hide the fact that his eyes were open so wide I feared they'd be locked in that position for the rest of his life. He was whipping his head from side to side, imagining, no doubt, the bear ripping through the nylon walls of the tent at any moment. I told him to stay put and wait. I headed off into the woods to collect the kids.

I am not a brave man. I can barely walk to the mailbox at night without skipping rapidly through the dark, whistling a tune called "I Am Totally Not Freaking Out Right Now" so that any hidden beasts are disinclined to attack. Heading off into the woods now was about as easy as giving myself a colonoscopy with a pair of binoculars.

I made it to the first homemade shelter. Erin and Alicia. The kids were quiet, asleep. I tried to wake them gently, without telling them about the bear. I said we were going back into camp, hoping to rouse them from sleep with as little panic as possible. Once they were fully awake, with their sleeping bags bundled in their arms, shoes on, I told them, as calmly as possible, that, yes, a bear had grabbed our food. The kids took it pretty well, most seeming rather excited at the prospect of sharing the woods with a bear.

We made it back into camp. There was no sign of Aaron until I got close to the tent.

"Aaron! What's up man?"

The zipper on the tent fly whipped up and Aaron's head popped out.

"The bear! He came back! He was here!" Aaron said, his voice high with giddy fear.

Apparently, Aaron had tried to brave it alone at the camp, standing out in the open to act as a beacon with his headlamp for me. The bear, whose tracks could be found the next day, cruised close enough to camp for Aaron to catch a glimpse of its reflecting eyes in his headlamp. It proved to be too much for him to handle, and he dove back into the tent.

Aaron pulled me aside. "Erik, the bear looked at me. He was looking right at me!" he said as he gripped my arm, trying to convey the terror of that moment.

What happened next is a series of vignettes lodged in my memory. Loudly walking and whistling through the dark forest, guiding sleepy kids back to Aaron's tent. My headlamp's beam bouncing around crazily, reminding me of every scene from *The Blair Witch Project*. During one of my trips back, I found the discarded backpack. The contents had partially spilled. The bear must've dropped the pack in its escape, or dug something out that was particularly appealing and taken it away. I debated whether or not to bring the bag back. It was, after all, what the bear was after. It also contained all our food, so giving it up seemed a poor alternative. I hauled the bag back to camp, and when I got there the kids were in a frenzy. The bear had returned, circling the camp and staying just beyond the reach of headlamps.

I headed out to collect my last batch of kids. Matthew, son of a German cinematographer, and Todd, a graceful, athletic kid whose sweetness and vulnerability was overshadowed by extreme video game addiction and a penchant for the kind of annoying behavior that makes a teacher want to take a two-by-four soaked in heavy-duty motor oil and whack the little shit upside the head. The boys were conked out in their shelter. Todd awoke in a panic, as he was a certifiable LA city kid whose fear of the dark, and the wilderness, had been apparent on this and many previous trips.

"Wha ... what?! Erik! What's going on?" Todd sputtered, raising himself on his elbows in his sleeping bag.

"Shhh, it's okay guys. We need to head back down into the main camp. A bear came into camp and tried to steal the food bag. We're all going to sleep down there."

Todd's eyes widened in the dark. He leapt out of his sleeping bag, grabbed the bag and a little Swiss Army knife, which I would find out later he slept with by his side. He was naked from the waist down.

"Let's go!" said Todd in a panic, clutching the knife and sleeping bag, clad in only a T-shirt. I watched his naked rear end begin running away through the woods.

"Todd, you don't have any pants on!"

"I've got all I need!" he said, and barefoot, he and Matthew began running back in the direction of camp.

Despite the dark, camp was easy to find at this point. I had told the kids that standard bear protocol states that in order to ward off a bear from camp, make a lot of noise. According to a report from Aaron when I returned, the bear had circled about a few times as I was off collecting Matthew and Todd. The kids were screaming, banging pots, and creating such a racket that I was pretty sure that all bears in a ten-mile radius heard them and ran the other way. I was able to get Todd to throw some shorts on, by the way, before he went down into a campsite full of adolescents all a-dangle. Poor kid never would've lived that down if he had.

I left Aaron with the kids and their cacophony, and headed far out into the forest and re-hung our food bag, not at all hopeful that it would work. It was well after midnight by the time I got back. The kids were all sacked out on the ground, in a tight circle, their heads facing in. Aaron said they had talked excitedly for a good while, and most were in high spirits. Nothing like a brush with Mother Nature to fuel a kid's sense of adventure, I thought.

The next morning I headed out early to retrieve the bag. Our ursine friend had indeed rediscovered the bag, and once again, despite my best efforts to the contrary, got it down from the tree. The bag was ripped and torn, and food was spread all over. The most interesting item was a jar of peanut butter. The cap seemed bitten, or, for all I know, screwed off using some clever Yogi the Bear trick. The bear had used its claws to scoop out the contents, and I could still clearly see the large marks of its claws in the bottom of the peanut butter jar. I imagined the bear sitting the way bears do when we imagine them as harmless teddys, on its butt, holding the jar between its legs and scooping out bite after bite of peanut butter, contently licking the goopy stuff off its claws.

17

Deadman Canyon

IN MY CAREFREE AND HAPHAZARD MID-TWENTIES, I PLANNED A RATHER extended and aggressive trek through the Sierras with my baker friend, Gordon, as part of a larger quest through the western United States. We had decided to take a few weeks of the summer and hike through Kings Canyon and Sequoia National Parks in California; drive over to the Grand Tetons in Wyoming for a few summit climbs; then bomb our way south and hike the slot canyons of Arizona. A two-month road trip, the kind you can only take before real job responsibilities, kids, bills, a mortgage, and the burden of participating in the hegemony of a capitalist society take over your life. Before you feel bad for not having nice shoes, for having to schlep your clothes to the laundromat instead of owning a nice under-over Kenmore. Before the idea of having gas station nachos for dinner seems suspect at best. Before you buy, at full retail price, the notion that life is to be *gotten on* with, rather than lived with careless abandon and a decided lack of financial stability.

That's why, when you're traveling around, you'll notice that rubber tramps who live in their trucks with a bunch of climbing gear tend toward their twenties and maybe early thirties; eventually, the breed dies out over time. While many graying silverbacks such as myself may glorify a life- style spent exploring the wild places in the world, a few nights sleeping rough in the back of a mid-size Toyota Tacoma would leave me crip- pled and downing ibuprofen like Skittles. But at the time Gordon and I were young, in our twenties, and tentatively employed. We struck out to explore the wilderness of the West, unencumbered by social status or any real engagement in industry or business.

Our first trip was into Sequoia National Park, where we planned to climb up over Elizabeth Pass, into a long glacial cleft called Dead Man's Canyon, and make our way into Kings Canyon National Park. I had been to the high country of the Sierra before, and was chattering nonsensically to the normally taciturn and stoic Gordon, who took turns driving with me from LA to the Sierras as I waxed poetic about the beauty of the Sierra.

In fact, I have a photo of Cynthia, my wife, from a trip we took with students to the area that I keep stuck in my wallet, creased and folded.

Have you ever fallen and *stayed* in love with someone because a photograph buttresses a memory so strongly it provides a kind of sustaining energy? The photo captures her against a snowy cliff face looming over the lake behind her. Her long dark hair is tied back in a handkerchief babushka-style. She looks like she could be a model for the label of some hippie-era applesauce.

Finances were tight for our Western adventure. I had so little money I didn't buy a proper road map or atlas (for the reader under thirty, maps are these large sheets of paper with a picture of roads and cities of a particular area used to navigate. Imagine Colorado taking a selfie). I grabbed one of those free tourist maps from a gas station and we were on our way, finally arriving at a visitors area replete with snack bar and small store stocked with items marked up to stroke-inducing prices. We were deep within the park, surrounded by cascading rivers and soaring sequoia.

We got our backcountry permits at a ranger station. The ranger on duty went through a list of questions designed, I believe, to ensure that visitors intent on heading into the vast, unpeopled ranges of the Sierra were doing so with a modicum of outdoor skills and wouldn't be found half starved a few days later. He asked me if I had purchased a map, meaning a USGS topographical map, or a guidebook at least, describing the trails and climbs we hoped to complete. I waved him off, saying we'd be fine with the map provided for free upon entrance to the park. Why spend money on an accurate map when you could depend on your hard-earned wilderness acumen?

The free map we used was sort of a cartoon map, with chubby bears cavorting along the edges rather than dragons and big, balloony, cartoonish writing. The scale was something like 1:1,000,000,000. I believe that the map covered the parks, as well as most of the western United States, and maybe the entire Pacific Rim. Up in the corner, there was a crude drawing of the sun and what appeared to be Mars. It was not, by any stretch of the amateur cartographers imagination, an accurate rendering of the landscape, nor a reliable guide to the mountainous country we were about to enter. But Gordon and I tramped off with the map nonetheless, equipped with only its brightly colored drawings to guide us.

We began the hike up into the high country, taking in the scenery. The High Sierras are remarkable, climbing among the giant sequoia, their massive, thick-barked red trunks seeming as solid as the earth they were fastened in. The trail canted up, and we were in highland meadows, with a cool high-altitude breeze chilling the sweat from the forested climb below. Blue sky stretched everywhere. High, rocky peaks were still covered in snow.

While I had visited the area before, we were heading up into the high country above the trees to a series of ridges and valleys where I'd never been. We came around a corner, and there it was. A marmot was just a few yards off the trail, happily munching grass and flowers. Its fat, sleek body gamboled this way and that, seeming remarkably spry for such a rotund little mammal. I shrieked in delight, like an eleven-year-old girl at a Harry Styles concert. Gordon, despite his Easter Island countenance, was also pleased, and flashed a rare smile. We snapped pictures, talking the whole time to the little ground-dweller, who seemed quite oblivious of our presence.

"Hey there, lil' guy! Who's a big fellow? Huh? You eatin' some flowers, buddy?" I crooned at the marmot.

After about fifteen minutes of wildlife viewing we moved on, excited and feeling quite fortunate to have had what was clearly a serendipitous run-in with a shy denizen of the alpine high country so soon. We had just started hiking when a man and woman came clomping down the trail toward us. I waved crazily at them, mouthing the word *marmot* and pantomiming a large rodent by holding my hands in front of me and blowing out my cheeks. Not wanting them to scare away the secretive creature, I motioned at them to stay quiet, pointing back over my shoulder with exaggerated motions and a maniacal smile. *Stay quiet, fellow travelers! Around the corner is a once-in-a-lifetime viewing experience!* They slowed as we passed, looking at me with a sort of weary curiosity.

"Psst! Hey, back there. A marmot! He's probably still there. Just off the trail. Check it out!" I said.

With tired, neutral expressions they walked on. Obviously not nature-lovers, I thought.

By the time the sun had set that evening, however, I had a firm understanding of our fellow hikers' disconsolate and bitter countenances.

There were marmots everywhere. While I was pitching the tent, one of them gnawed a hole in the rainfly I had cast off a few feet behind me. A fat, cheeky little bastard stole a packet of oatmeal out of my bag. One of them chewed a hole in Gordon's boot-tongue. There was a burrow right near our tent, and the beasts squealed and made a racket all night long, making sleep impossible. You couldn't turn around without being face to face with ten pounds of alpine rodent. One even chased a pine marten through our camp, a carnivore that looks like a cross between a fox and a weasel. These marmots were tough, skullduggerous little buggers, and our camp was overrun with them. Before long my Attenborough-esque appreciation had given way to keen annoyance and petulant griping. The couple we saw hiking had probably, as we did, spent the night battling the bloody creatures, and our awe at the first sighting was probably the emotional equivalent of salt in the wound.

Gordon and I hiked up over Elizabeth Pass the next day. We were not prepared in a number of ways—including the fact that I was trying to gauge distances using the cartoon map—which would ultimately lead to a somewhat desperate situation. By the time we got to Elizabeth Pass, we were exhausted. The pass was just over eleven thousand feet, and the thin air and altitude sucked the energy from us and left us wheezing and bent over our knees.

We could look down into Dead Man's Canyon, a wide, long, sweeping valley that stretched into the distance. The entire upper part of the valley was a huge melting snowfield. We stopped at the top of the pass, black spots of exertion and altitude popping in front of our eyes. Gordon and I ate lunch, then leaned back among the rocks to rest in the sunshine before the descent into the canyon.

We fell asleep. Or passed out, depending on how you look at it. Leaning against our packs, our heads wobbling on our necks like balloons, we succumbed to the oxygen deprivation and the previous night's marmot-induced sleeplessness experiment and took way too long of a nap. Upon waking, we realized a good chunk of the day had passed, and we needed to hustle to get down past the snow to camp for the night.

We headed out across the snowfield toward the cleft of the canyon, the early summer sun blazing overhead. We were post-holing every step, our feet crunching through the snow to the rocks underneath, falling through the crusty layer of snow sometimes up to our waists. We hadn't anticipated that much snow, because anticipation and planning had not had room in our overly enthused brains, which were occupied by testosterone and impatience. Our boots were quickly soaked, and our legs cut up by the sharp, crusty snow.

We eventually got down into the shady canyon. And the problems began in earnest.

I grew up in Vermont. I'm used to mosquitoes and blackflies. While not a huge fan of the blood-sucking insects of the world, I believed I had a solid tolerance and wouldn't let a few winged annoyances derail a trip through a place as sublimely beautiful as the Sierra high country. I thought I was relatively inured to their sanguine advances. I believed I knew what "buggy" meant, as in, "How was the hike?" "Gorgeous, just a bit buggy." I was wrong.

The mosquitoes in Dead Man's Canyon were huge, fierce, and brutal. As we began picking our way through the rocky scree that had, for millennia, eroded down the high canyon sides and scattered across the canyon floor, we realized we had neglected to bring bug repellent of any kind. The trail wove in and out of trees, and the high ridges on either side shaded the canyon almost entirely. Water flowed everywhere, both from the snowfield up by the pass and down the canyon walls. It was perfect mosquito habitat: lots of standing water, cool, shady. The mosquitoes attacked en masse like they hadn't eaten in weeks. They feasted on our backs, our necks, both on exposed flesh and through our T-shirts and shorts. I turned to tell Gordon that we needed to get the heck out of there, leave the boggy, wet place we were in. His hat had legions of gray, hungry mosquitoes perched on it, and he had a least a dozen little vampires hunched on his face, busily probing his cheeks with their sharp proboscises. It was like a scene from a horror movie.

I came up with an idea that I thought was intelligent, well-thought-out wisdom born out of years of outdoor experience.

"Run!" I shouted, slapping at my own face reflexively after seeing Gordon's host of bloodsuckers.

We began sprinting down the trail, waving our arms madly and trying to hold off the growing swarms of bugs. It was horrible. They got in my ears, along the hairline right at the back of my neck.

"Gordon! High ground, where there's a breeze!" I screamed, veering off the trail and starting to scramble up the boulder field toward the high canyon wall. Gordon, who I could tell was resigning himself to death, or perhaps just losing consciousness due to blood loss, weakly followed, not even bothering to slap at the mosquitoes that were sucking at his eyebrows, his nose, and his temples.

We didn't get far up the steep canyon wall, mainly because it was a steep canyon wall and we weren't fucking mountain goats. And it didn't matter, as there was no breeze up there anyway. The swarm followed us. We started back down the slope, which consisted of large blocks of rock that had tumbled down the walls. As I neared the bottom, back toward the trail, I heard a snap behind me among Gordon's labored breaths and scrabbling, scraping footsteps. I didn't hear any footsteps after that. I turned, and Gordon was sitting, staring down at his ankle, which was wedged between two sharp slabs of rock.

"That was my ankle," he said, referring to the snapping noise.

I helped Gordon hobble back to the trail. The bugs were really bad now, getting in our eyes, their insistent and maddening whine saturating the air. Gordon's hat was coated in a gray felt composed entirely of insects. I'm sure mine looked the same. I had somehow lost the trail. Gordon couldn't walk at more than a pained, aggrieved shuffle, his face grimacing in agony when he limped on the hurt ankle. At least I think he grimaced. His face was obscured by thousands of whirling, whining insects.

"Let's pitch the tent!" I shouted. We were out of water, our mouths pasty and dry. I set up our little two-man tent in record speed, and muddy, exhausted, and bitten, we collapsed inside. I managed to fill our water bottles from the stream nearby, and treated the water with iodine tablets. No time for pumping water through a purifier. I'd be sucked of all my blood in minutes. The hoard of insects settled in a thick gray mat, furring the screened door of our tent, waiting for us to emerge. We climbed into our bags, muddy and lost and wet, to sleep. We stared out at the darkening forest, welts raising on every inch of skin. Exhausted, hungry, and seriously questioning the logic of outdoor activities in general, we fell asleep.

I woke in the morning and for a moment forgot where I was. Rolling over and catching sight of Gordon, I thought I'd had too much to drink the night before and had a one-night stand with the Elephant Man. But it was just Gordon, still comatose in his bag. His face was swollen with bites, his eyebrows especially puffy, making him look slightly Neanderthal-ish and dim.

We roused ourselves and inspected his ankle. We had not raised it, or wrapped it, the night before, and thus his body's natural protective swelling and inflammation had advanced unabated through the night. Gordon's lower leg looked like a pink python that had mistakenly swallowed a volleyball. The joint was enormous and grotesquely swollen. He winced at the slightest movement, and looked at it with a strange mixture of resignation, horror, and remove, as though such a disgusting thing couldn't possibly belong to him.

Though barely dawn, the bugs were back out. They were all perched on our screen, waiting, patiently yet malevolently, huffing our exhaled CO_2 in the hopes that we'd emerge to become breakfast. Which, of course, I'd have to. I had to go find the trail that I'd lost in our mad dash the night before.

We figured we were close to what was labeled as a "Ranger Station" on our map, highlighted by a cartoon of a smiling female ranger in shorts sniffing a flower next to a log cabin. Help was near, I hoped, as I wasn't sure how, exactly, we were going to move Gordon. His ankle looked very likely to be broken. He couldn't walk on it, couldn't put weight on it.

I sprinted out in the early morning, wildly waving my hands around as I cast about for the trail. I found it. Back at the tent, we wrapped T-shirts around our faces and necks. Wore long sleeves and pants, though the temperature was climbing. We couldn't wrap Gordon's ankle—our med kit didn't have the right stuff—but he wore a double pair of socks and we tied his boot laces as tight as he could stand it to immobilize the joint. I shifted as much weight as possible into my pack from Gordon's, and we scurried off as fast as his ankle would let us.

Luckily, we cleared the swampy section relatively quickly, and that, plus a strong, beaming June sun, spread the little bloodsuckers thinner and thinner. We made it to the ranger station, which by its unkempt appearance had last housed a ranger during the late 1970s. The windows were shuttered fast, and the door was locked with a brutal and large clasplock. Looking at my Looney Toons map, as Gordon soaked his hideous ankle in the freezing, snowmelt waters of a river that ran along in front of the vacant ranger cabin, I realized that we were a solid dozen miles, in any direction we chose, from the nearest road. Whatever we did, it would have to involve some other way of moving about, as Gordon could barely walk, and the exertions of the brief jaunt that morning had already put him in considerable pain. The closest place where I felt I could reliably find help was a big campground and ranger station deep in Kings Canyon National Park. It was up and over a break in the mountains called Hurricane Gap, and it looked to be about ten miles, though I was beginning to be suspicious of the reliability of my map.

Gordon and I talked it out and decided that I'd head up over the gap to get help. My thought was that I would commandeer a mule or two, as I knew there were pack trains that crisscrossed the mountains. I figured it was standard protocol in the mountains, and some code of the outdoors would entitle me to a little donkey or two to get Gordon out of the woods.

I packed light and headed up into the gap. I left Gordon with the tent, food, and the stove. He sat at the river, floating his ankle in the water and looking rather forlorn. After a few hours of hiking, I began to approach the open V of blue sky that was the apex of my journey; the rest, as would be blessedly welcome, was downhill. As I hurried up the hill, concerned about getting up and over and down into the next valley where the road, campsite, and ranger station was, my breath came in harsh, ragged, altitudinal gasps. I could hear and feel the blood pounding in my head. I felt tired and dehydrated.

One of the things you quickly realize about hiking long distances is that at first the long stretches of time with nothing to do but plod on stir deep thoughts about the meaning of life. Quickly, though, as you tire, you begin to focus exclusively and obsessively on fantasies involving large, carbohydrate-laden meals and putting your feet up. It's only after the whole ordeal is over that you realize the meaning of life *is* eating carbohydrate-laden meals with your feet up.

The bear surprised me. I was hiking up a steep slope, hands on my thighs, staring only at the ground at my feet. Briefly looking up, there it was, coming down the slope. A shaggy, cinnamon-colored bear. We passed each other in broad daylight, no more than thirty feet apart.

I'm not going to get metaphysical and spiritual here. I'm not looking to star in Herzog's *Grizzly Man 2*. But I will say this. I passed a sentient being. We were so much the same, both mountain commuters with pressing business to attend to. When that bear looked at me and our eyes met, I didn't see the cold and fierce gaze. There was a self-awareness there I found familiar. I saw a creature that I could relate to despite our obvious differences. Like if we could just sit down for a while with a beer, we could reach a friendly understanding, a shared mountain-trekker camaraderie. I know that we're different on an evolutionary continuum—that in terms of cranial capacity, tool use, language acquisition, and the ability to get through a *New York Times* article all the way to the end, we are separate and distinct beings—but in that moment, I had this feeling that the bear understood me and I it. I had the sense I was in the presence of a thoughtful creature.

The bear's expression was a slightly hurried, commuter-on-a-busy train sort of glance. For the brief moment we locked eyes, it was not unlike the unintentional eye contact one makes with another diner in a restaurant, a slight emotional double-take that flickers in a stranger's eye when you hold their gaze for a disconcerting and socially unacceptable long time, followed rapidly by a flash of awkwardness when you quickly look down to study the menu with the focus of a rabbi studying the Torah. I think we were both a bit embarrassed, is what I'm trying to say. I think the bear was as surprised as I was at the unexpected meeting, and we both decided to keep going about our business in an attempt to gloss over the embarrassing inter-species moment.

And then it was over. The bear continued on its journey down into Dead Man's Canyon, and I headed up over the pass. The next day, I would discover that the same bear walked by Gordon as he sat in camp. Gordon, however, did not attempt to commune with the beast, but scrambled into the tent to hide. Which is something I've never understood. If a bear wants at you, I'm guessing the least formidable defense is a millimeter of nylon between you and 250 pounds of angry ursine rage.

I made it to the campground at nightfall. I headed directly to the ranger station. I clomped up onto the porch, where a mustachioed, sinewy, and graying ranger met me at the door. The parking lot, store, and campsites behind me were filled with loud, noisy people, barbecuing, talking, laughing. RV air conditioners hummed. It was bizarre, to have been so remote that morning, and now to be amid the chaos of vacationing America. I won't say I wasn't relieved.

The ranger patiently explained to me that the mules I was requesting would cost $450 for a day and a night. Plus guide fees, as they didn't just hand out mules to people who said they had friends who had busted an ankle. I was shocked. I assumed that was what rangers did; they ranged about, looking for people to save.

"What do you mean, I have to pay? My friend is hurt. His ankle is probably broken. Isn't it your job to go and help him get out?"

"No," the skinny ranger said.

I was also told that I could airlift Gordon out with a local helicopter service for the bargain-basement price of $4,500. I passed.

They finally took pity on me. I suppose I was kind of pathetic, ascribing to modern rangers a sort of backcountry ethic that only exists in movies. The whole point is to not take unnecessary risks, so you don't get in a jam you can't get yourself out of. The rangers explained to me that it was the responsibility of the backcountry trekker to figure out how to get out of the wilderness, unless it was a real emergency, which, apparently, a busted ankle is not. I was somewhat appalled, but also understood the logic. If they rescued every jackass like me who went into the backcountry unprepared, then all the jackasses like me would think it was okay to go out there and mess around without taking into account the consequences, knowing that the rangers would swoop in and save them if needed.

The rangers told me I could raid their first-aid supply closet and food pantry, and sleep on their porch without having to pay an overnight fee. I felt, oddly, beholden to them. Though I had imagined myself returning to Gordon at the head of a train of mules packed with vittles, waving a beaten cowboy hat in the air in greeting and hunkering down to a crackling fire to fix up some varmint stew, ready to haul him out donkey-style, I had to accept crutches, some splints, various wraps and instant chemical ice packs, and some MREs (Meals Ready to Eat), surplus army food in big plastic blocks that tasted like big plastic blocks.

I hiked out early the next morning, back over the pass. We took two days to get out, wrapping Gordon's ankle in a splint and ACE bandages and having him limp out on crutches. It turned out, they informed us at the hospital, that Gordon had a largish fracture but didn't need a cast. We continued our epic summer quest undeterred, visiting the Tetons and various points east of Los Angeles. We drank beer a lot more than we hiked due to Gordon's ankle, but with such a tale to regale our fellow imbibers with, it was a pleasant enough summer after all. And that bear, somehow, in the most surprising moments, is still with me.

18

The Storm of the Sierra

There is no way to happiness—happiness is the way.
                                    —THICH NHAT HANH

SPENDING TIME IN THE WILDERNESS IS A UNIQUE WAY TO MAKE A STAND as an individual. "I will not smell good!" "I will eat freeze-dried lasagna!" "I will poop in a hole!"

Our campsite was in a little patch of flat next to a small, teardrop-shaped glacial lake surrounded by the concave wall of a large cirque. The trees were entirely conifers and none were all that tall—most maybe twenty to thirty feet high. We weren't that far below the treeline, where altitude makes flora stunted and runty.

I always set up my trips with specific roles assigned to specific students. The kid in charge of washing the dishes was the Teflon Knight; the kid in charge of the trowel and precious stock of toilet paper was named Stink-Bottom Johnson. I did my usual speech about Leave No Trace camping ethics. We made dinner. Martin—who I'd hired to help with trips based on the recommendation of a friend—was generally helpful, but there seemed to be moments when things got a bit dizzying for him, when the constant adolescent chatter and movement made him nauseous. He was rail thin and small, with a scrubby, Brillo-pad beard and a hat it looked like he'd picked up from a street vendor in South America. He would disappear from view and return with a look of resolve.

I pitched a tent for Sarah, the teacher of the class who had hired me to take her students up into the Sierra. She'd become something of a mentor to me. In her fifties, Sarah was acerbic and funny and committed to education and learning. She swore like a sailor while watching March Madness, yet wore flowy, linen clothing. An enigmatic woman who even offered me a place to stay when I was between apartments (read: broke) and became something of a mother figure.

Some of the kids were in tents. The rest were in two groups, sleeping bags spread on two tarps. I got the kids settled in as night fell. Sarah went to her tent. It was getting dark. I grabbed the monstrously heavy pack I had filled with all our food and went to hang it out of the reach of enterprising bears. Walking away from camp, I came upon Martin. He'd strung a hammock, a flimsy-looking thing, between two trees.

"Going hammock style, huh?" I asked.

"Yeah," he said with a sweaty grin. He surveyed his hammock with a look of accomplishment.

"That's cool," I said, still walking by him.

"Got it in Thailand," he said. *Yeah*, I thought. *That and a case of the clap.*

I headed out into the woods, and heard him shuffle step in behind me. We had trouble finding a good tree. They all had dense branches down low, making climbing them difficult. None of them seemed to have good, solid, horizontal branches high enough. It was getting darker and darker. My headlamp's glow wasn't very strong. Martin had a small black flashlight in his fist. We finally settled on a tall, gnarled pine tree. It didn't have a very good variety of branches. Night was falling, and the wind was picking up. We got the bag half hung, half lodged high up in the tree. After all, what were the chances of yet another bear stealing my food, I thought. I said good night and headed back to camp.

The kids were all tucked in, fat polypropylene sausages rolling about on the outspread tarps. The tents—Sarah's and the few students who'd opted out of a star-gazing slumber al fresco on the ground—were lit up from within. The soft wind was picking up, and the pines around our heads shushed and clattered as their branches swayed.

I remembered a time when Sarah had been asked to deal with a particularly disruptive student. The kid had been really out of control in the classroom, and Sarah was called to take him outside and figure out what to do. I was crossing from one building to the next, and saw that she'd brought him to the edge of campus. The kid was using a flattened cardboard box to slide down a steep embankment. Again and again, this kid would run to the top of the hill and whip down, crashing spectacularly every time at the bottom, only to come racing back up to the top to do it again, grinning from ear to ear. Sarah was standing calmly by, offering a few words of encouragement now and again. As I walked by, she smiled mischievously and shrugged.

I shoved my body into my beaten blue sleeping bag, heaving myself about in the time-honored ritual of trying to get comfortable on the hard, rocky ground. You roll over onto your side and find a few moments of peace, but then notice a wickedly cold draft seeping down between your shoulder blades. So you roll over to pull tight the gap in your sleeping bag, losing the precious position. You try lying on your stomach, but a rock is digging into your belly, so you lie on your back, open-mouthed, and the high dry air parches your tongue into a piece of leather. Now you notice that your sock is falling down, annoyingly clumped around the arch of your foot, but the condom-like fit of your sleeping bag prevents you from bending down to pull it up, despite your best *America's Got Talent* contortionist act. Soon enough, breathing heavily and now completely twisted in your goose down–filled Patagonia straightjacket, you succumb to the futility of comfort and sleep and enter a void of numb, sleepless misery.

I rested. But I rested in the way you sleep on the first night of a backpacking trip. Which is to say: terribly. I'd sort of pass out, falling into a thoughtless fugue listening to the nice hum of the wind, only to begin obsessing over the fact that the place I had chosen to lay my bag was inclined the wrong way, ever so slightly—my feet were millimeters above my head. I began to stress that the blood would run down and pool in my brain. Then I'd fall asleep again, but on my arm, which would wake me up later as a flopping, electrified appendage. I'd grasp it and move the dead weight of it about, fearing that I'd done permanent nerve damage by letting my arm fall asleep. Then, once the pins and needles began to subside, I'd start to sleep again, only to realize that I had to piss. Badly? Not sure. But there was definitely piss somewhere in my bladder. Maybe I should. But I wouldn't. Maybe I could hold it. Maybe not. And on went the night.

The wind picked up, and began a not so subtle climb in register and decibel. I began to worry that this might be more than just a run-of-the-mill breeze; summer storms in the Sierra are quick and decisive.

The wind had reached an intense pitch only a bit later when I heard it. A faint *Tink! Tink! Tink, tink, tink!* It went on and on. Though it was hard to tell due to the wind, I thought it was coming from where Martin had stretched his hammock. I willed myself to ignore it and go back to sleep.

Tink! Tink! Tink, tink, tink, tink! It was growing ever more consistent and, if my ears could be trusted, insistent. I squirmed out of my bag, softly cursing in the dark and casting about for my boots.

I headed over toward Martin's camp. I could see the blue of his flashlight in the dark. *Tink! Tink!* As I grew closer, I realized that in the dark I'd misjudged. Martin was nowhere near his hammock. He was deeper into the trees. He was near where we'd hung the bear bag.

I found him in the dark near the tree where our food was hung. He held a spoon and a small tin cup in his hand. He was looking upward, his little black flashlight in his hand and a lamp on his head. He was rapping the little tin cup with his spoon, his neck cords straining as he stared up into the tree. He looked somehow like a plucked bird, the skin of his neck goose-bumped.

A bear sat comfortably in the tree. The pack containing all our food was cradled in its arms. In a bear hug, really. The bear was nosing about the top of the bag, sitting there twenty-five feet up in the pine tree I'd chosen. Despite how close we were, it seemed to care not at all about us. It wasn't a massive beast at all, more like a large, overfed sixth grader in a woolly suit. I watched as the animal dipped its head, and I heard the tough, Cordura nylon of the pack rip as the bear grabbed the fabric in its teeth.

"Supposed to scare the bear away with noise," said Martin, plinking and plunking his little cup. His face was frozen in an expression of fear. There was a wide expanse of white around his irises.

"It doesn't look scared," I said.

Martin turned to me. "No."

Martin kept tinking and plinking. I jogged back to camp, my head-lamp bouncing along rocks and trees. The wind was a steady jet-engine whine. I came back with the big guns—a large cooking pot and a softball-sized rock. Martin stared in fascination, or blank fear, as I passed by him. I got right to the base of the tree and drew my arm back.

The first strike of the rock on the pot sounded like a tinny cannon. The sound boomed out, way more effective than I'd thought. I felt, more than heard or saw, Martin jump behind me. The bear was in my head-lamp's wavering beam. It chuffed loudly, the pack falling and piling up beside the tree as it disgorged its contents in a jumbled mess. As I gonged the pot again and again, the bear suddenly jerked and darted, then was smashing and flailing down the tree. Branches snapped and the whole tree shook. I was standing at the base, right in the bear's path. The beast bombed toward me headfirst.

I screamed and flailed backward, knocking into Martin and dropping the pot. I fell on my butt, legs askew, as the bear barreled right down the tree and ran, just a few feet from me, away into the dark. My lungs were tight, and I was absolutely frozen in fear.

"What the fuck did you do that for! Fuck!" Martin was yelling, and his voice sounded like one more chord in the symphony of evolutionary panic in my head. The adrenaline ebbed, and I briefly wondered if I'd laid a fright-turd in my pants. Chances were good.

"That bear almost landed on you!" Martin said. I sat on the ground for a good few minutes, earnestly willing my heart to start beating again. Eventually I was able to stand, and Martin and I gathered up the pack and its spilled contents. We huddled closer than necessary in the dark. We moved quickly, and our breath was hurried.

Martin volunteered to get the bag up into a new tree. We headed away from camp as far as we dared in the dark, not wanting to bring the bear back around if we could help it.

A piercing and efficient rain began to fall. Lighting began to flash. We heard thunder boom as we selected a tree, and again, louder this time, as Martin began to climb. The storm was coming down.

Martin was trying to shimmy a tree in the dark, headlamp illuminating a trunk covered in thick, vicious, barb-like branches. He held his little black flashlight in his teeth. The food pack sloughed back and forth, dropping random packages of food. It rocked on his back like a gigantic sock full of marbles. I wondered how much food lay around in the dark on the ground that we hadn't been able to find.

Lightning split the sky, followed by a hollow, booming thunder. I shrieked a little shriek, unmanly but necessary. Rain began pounding down, and the lightning continued flashing. At one point, it struck so close that I smelled the ozone. I was beginning to think Martin was going to be lit up like a Christmas ornament.

But he wasn't. He got the bag hung, somehow, and tree-hugged the trunk all the way down. We ran humped over like Morlocks back to Martin's hammock, rain pelting us all the way. It dawned on me that half the kids were sleeping outside in this nasty storm. I hoped they were okay. I was soaked.

I ran all the way back to camp in the dark, my headlamp bouncing off trees as the rain pelted down. "Get the kids in the tents!" I heard Sarah yell. I began piling kids into tents, exceeding their sleeping capacities by multiple factors, the kids screaming and yelling and basically having fun with it all. It was chaos—the mud, the rain, the flashing lightning and booming thunder, soaked kids, and me running around witless and hoping that Martin hadn't been electrocuted somewhere back in the trees.

Within the next year Sarah would get sick, pneumonia, which would travel to her lungs. She died, only in her fifties—not much older than I am now. That such a person could just wink out of existence shocked me to my core. There she was, and then there she wasn't, and my memories of her began to take on the shape of half-remembered scenes from movies.

I gave Sarah's eulogy at the service hosted by the school. It was a really, really bad eulogy, and she deserved better. But I tried to be so deep, so meaningful, that it came out sounding ridiculous. I have since thrown away the copy of the speech, but I remember the first line. *We are mired in our collective grief, today.* Mired? Sarah was probably turning in her grave when she heard that. Pretentious crap, I could imagine her saying.

I finally got all the kids stuffed into tents. I was beyond wet, and plodded over to Sarah's tent. "You okay in there?" I yelled. I could hear what sounded like wheezing and coughing. The altitude could affect anyone, and I began to worry Sarah was having some kind of medical issue. Was she asthmatic? I realized I'd never asked.

"Sarah! You okay?" No response. I unzipped the tent, shining my light in.

Sarah was sitting there on her sleeping bag, laughing and laughing and laughing.

19

Güero

The Gringo, locked into the fiction of white superiority . . .
—GLORIA E. ANZALDÚA

OUR RIDE PICKED US UP AT THE MANZANILLO AIRPORT, WHICH IS A single runway paved right into the dunes along the beach. He was driving an old, beat-up fourteen-passenger van, an ugly golden brown that looked like metallized shit. We clambered in, and the kids, dutiful little Americans that they were, began searching for seatbelts.

"*No hay!*" our driver called jovially from the front seat. The kids looked back at him as he laughed at their combination of dismay, shock, and creeping pleasure at doing something that had been ingrained as potentially lethal. I reached to shut the sliding door of the van. Just like the seatbelts, it appeared the mechanism that locked the door shut was also nonexistent, so the door was open as he pulled away from the curb.

We were off. The joy, for a thirteen-year-old, of riding seatbelt-less in a speeding van along Mexican highways with the door open is not to be underestimated.

We passed the shrunken and shriveled bodies of a few desiccated cows along the side of the highway. Even in this small detail, it was plain to see just how hermetically sealed most kids' lives were. They gawked and exclaimed "*Ew! Gross!*" as we passed them, but in reality, that's a commonplace scene the world over. That and the trash that littered the roadside.

Manzanillo is a port city on the Pacific side of Mexico. About halfway down the length of the country, the city is situated around a large harbor. While there is some tourism there—the beaches are lined with big hotels and palm-frond cabanas—it's not like Acapulco or Cancun. There are no ruins nearby or other tourism locales, and it's not really a backpacker's hotspot. Manzanillo is probably most well known as the place where Bo Derek and Dudley Moore capered about in the late 1970s film *10*. Ironically, Manzanillo is where Mexicans go for holiday, to escape the hordes of *gabachos* invading their beaches.

I was in Manzanillo with a group of middle schoolers from Los Angeles to take them snorkeling in the great Pacific. While I had some experience with exploring reefs and snorkeling in the open ocean, my experience with international travel was minimal. I had been to Mexico a few times, but all my trips were short and embarrassingly shallow. Road trips from Los Angeles down to Baja, mostly, the highlights of which included getting stumble-drunk at Papas and Beer in Ensenada and eating a generous serving of hallucinogenic mushrooms on Rosarito Beach.

In fact, at one point in these early forays south of the border, I drank Malcolm Lowry–esque amounts of alcohol at a beachside bar and wandered away into the town without paying my tab. I befriended two mangy street dogs and fed them tacos. Returning to my hotel, I was met by the *federales*. They demanded payment for my bar bill and then some lest I go to jail, which took every cent I had. I drove back north across the border the next day, my car running on fumes and my head a noxious balloon. I had single-handedly confirmed every stereotype of the exploitive, obnoxious gringo.

What I never thought about visiting Mexico was the tapestry of drama that was unfolding around me. When America finally views history outside the prism of whiteness, she'll see that the mass migration of Mexican and Central American families is a great tapestry of heroic struggle and sacrifice comparable to the tales of the pioneers and early settlers we venerate in folklore and popular culture. The Joads with melanin. When we see that migrant Americans *are* Americans, we can incorporate that story and be emboldened by it. Look at a map. Trace your finger from the Mexican state of Guerrero north through the Sonoran Desert, past cities plagued by violent *buchons*, toward the border. The journey is epic, the tragedy heart-wrenching, the adventure real. All of this was lost on me when I was a young man in my twenties, however.

I found a grimy dock the day after we arrived, with a dingy boat tied up alongside it. Using a combination of strained smiles, arm waving, and made-up Spanglish: *"El snorkel?" "Aqua azul?" "El reef del coral?"* I tried to convince the captain to take us out on the water. I had been directed there by the man from whom we'd rented our little house—a poured concrete affair with small, echoey rooms. I dropped the man's name and received not even a flicker of recognition. Meanwhile, two silent crew members had appeared and watched the proceedings with inscrutable faces. Eventually, after a few minutes of jaw-breaking, desperate grins and constant reassurances to the kids, who were growing anxious at the stalemate, I received a curt nod from the captain. Registering this as a success, I then settled in to discuss price. How much would it cost to take a dozen-plus kids and a few adults snorkeling? We bantered a bit—and by we, I mean me.

I had picked up, somewhere, that it was considered rude *not* to barter. Having no idea what the going rate is for snorkeling in the Pacific was a challenge, so I threw out amounts that were either ridiculously low or high. I received no reaction whatsoever. I stuttered and waved pesos about and set back Mexican American diplomatic relations by about thirty years. The captain stared at me with a mixture of stern forbearance mixed with fatigue. Finally, no doubt embarrassed for me, he offered a curt nod, at which his crew began to move about the boat, and we loaded ourselves onto the deck as the diesel engines coughed into life. In retrospect I realize I looked like a colonial-era, red-faced Englishman trying to bribe the local chief out of a few thousand square miles of waterfront property. It is not one of my prouder moments.

Once on board, flush with success from my cultural immersion experiment, I looked around. The boat didn't look like a tourist vessel—it looked like a work boat, with a layer of grime that I associated with authenticity. I didn't note any snorkeling gear, or ice chest full of bottled water, or anything, really, to suggest that this was a craft used for visiting tourists. I interpreted this as evidence that we'd found the real deal, and escaped the catered and "soft" tourist-trap outfits plying the waters of the bay. These were the local guys, the down and dirty no-frills outfit that would take us out to the really sweet spots only locals knew about—past all the namby-pamby tourists paddling around in fluorescent neoprene to where the real Mexicans snorkeled and spearfished for octopus and red snapper. Heck, I figured they'd probably bring us to some local beach party afterward, where we'd roast some freshly caught sea bass over mesquite fires, eat delicious fish tacos smoking hot from the flames with some salt and lime while the captain's kind, gentle wife cracked open a fresh aloe leaf and spread the cooling gel on my sun-sore shoulders. A guitar would be plunked and beers opened, the sun would set, cross-cultural laughter and conviviality would ensue.

The boat motored along for a bit—maybe fifteen minutes—and then the captain cut the engine. The whole time, the kids I had brought grew more and more apprehensive. The shoreline receded, and we headed out into the bay. The water had yet to take on that aqua-blue color that graces advertisements for Sandals resorts. Instead, it was murky. Not just murky, but downright oily. Manzanillo—I'd later discover—is the busiest port in Mexico, delivering all the goods by sea destined for Mexico City. It is, in essence, an industrial port, and as such the waters are covered by a thick, rainbow layer of oil and fuel. To the north is Santiago Bay, a renowned snorkeling spot that I would find out about after the trip, where there is even a famous shipwreck to explore. We, however, were not in Santiago Bay. We were in the main sea lanes for container-ship and tanker traffic. Huge, rust-scabbed container ships floated in the distance. Grim-looking fishing boats crossed the horizon with massive purse-seine nets.

The boat rocked silently on the waves. The captain came out from the wheelhouse. He stared at me cryptically.

"Is this the reef?" I asked. The water surrounding the boat was black and heaved with a sloshing, turgid weight.

"*Sí*," he said.

Now, I was not a seasoned snorkeler—I'd only done it a few times—but I was pretty sure we weren't at a reef. The two deckhands came up, silently flanking the captain.

"Okay. Well then."

I looked at the kids. Snorkeling among brightly colored fish had been one of the things they'd been most excited about. They didn't look excited about this—whatever "this" was. I realize that scamming a *güero* is a karmic form of comeuppance in recompense for El Norte's imperialist treatment of our southern neighbor, but it still stung. There was, however, nothing for it.

"I'll give it a shot. Who wants to jump in with me?"

There were no takers. One of the impassive crew brought out a plastic bucket. In it were two old, mildewed masks with snorkels. I decided there was no way in hell I was putting that hose in my mouth.

I shucked my shirt, grabbed a mask, and hoisted myself onto the gunwales, legs swinging over the side. Underneath my burnt, crab-red legs the water bobbed black and ominously. I shoved off the side and plunged into the drink. While I treaded water and tried to get the mask on, the smell and taste of diesel invaded my mouth and nose. I got the mask fitted and began swimming away from the boat in slow strokes. I tentatively put my face in the water, and stared down into the black abyss.

Actually, I have no idea if it was an abyss. I couldn't see more than a few feet. The water was thick and murky. I began to lose some of my fear, and began replacing it with anger. I paddled around, looking for a reef. None. Never even saw the bottom. The water was dark and shadowed, broken only by little blobs of light and the occasional shaft of sunlight. I circled more and more widely away from the boat.

"Anything?" yelled one of the kids.

"Not yet," I said with false cheer.

I began to realize, with slow and embarrassing clarity, how badly we'd been duped. I then wondered: If they weren't a legitimate snorkeling outfit, who did I just leave my students with, floating a few miles offshore in the Pacific Ocean? I tore my mask off and tried to see the boat—figure out what was going on.

That's when I felt the first sting.

Jellyfish—small, golf ball–sized, translucent ones—were floating around me. One, two, three, I spotted. My leg burned where I'd been stung—an electric, pinpoint ache. I pressed the mask to my face and looked underwater around me. Four, five, six, seven; I stopped counting. The little jellies were everywhere. Another sting on my lower back. They were uncomfortable, somewhere lower on the scale than a wasp but higher than a mosquito, but there were many of them between me and the boat.

"Do you see the reef?" one of the kids called.

"No, just jellyfish. I'm coming back."

I began to swim back toward the boat. Another sting, this one on the inside of my arm right by the elbow. I began to swim in that wide-eyed, frenzied fashion anyone who's seen the *Jaws* franchise movies appreciates. Big, splashing arm movements, neck arched and head held high. Rapid, shallow breaths sounding like a cross between a wheeze and a whine. In my head I wondered how many toxic stings it would take before I was paralyzed and would sink beneath the waves, drift down into the deep in my saggy swim trunks. The boat engine rumbled to life, and a cloud of noxious black diesel smoke drifted over the water. There was a moment of panic as I thought they intended to leave me there, floating in a minefield of jellyfish. I believe I uttered a high-pitched approximation of "Wait!" which sounded like a donkey that just got stung by a wasp on its testicles. I finally clambered aboard, hurling my body out of the water. The captain still looked deadpan.

"No reef," I said, breathing hard. Then used one of my few words of Spanish, said with as much venom as I could muster. "No *pescado*."

The captain changed expression, for the first time. He looked a bit thoughtful. "No," he said. "*Pero muchas medusas.*"

I looked up the words in the Spanish-English dictionary I had brought when we got back that afternoon. "No," the captain had offered philosophically. "But plenty of jellyfish."

20

Sk8 or Die

I can't remember where I saw it, or who owned the chunky VHS tape, but at some point in my adolescence I sat down and watched *The Search for Animal Chin*, a ridiculous and fantastic DIY skateboarding video starring the Bones Brigade, a group of skaters—some of them barely older than me at the time—such as Tony Hawk, Rodney Mullen, and Steve Caballero.

Chin is a gonzo movie. Check it out. It's weird and never takes itself seriously, but highlights the sort of rebellious attitude that skateboarding has both embraced and rejected, commodified and sold over decades. It was a bunch of kids skating where they shouldn't, breaking rules, and thrashing the cityscape. I loved it.

So I, too, began skateboarding, despite the fact that in Vermont concrete was hard to come by. I begged my parents to buy me a skateboard, which they did, and my father and I constructed a ramp. I knew nothing about actual ramp building, and neither did my father. The frame was made of old cedar fence posts, the bark still on them. The deck of the ramp, which was not concave as most ramps are but flat and angled precipitously upward, was a large eight-by-four-foot piece of particle board. The thing probably weighed about a ton. It was gnarled and seemed like the sort of ramp australopithecines would've used.

I set it up on the old cracked and lumpy driveway of an orchard next door to the house I grew up in. This wasn't the urban skate scene I think most of us imagine when we think of skateboarding: graffiti-covered alleyways and concrete jungle-type cityscapes. This was rural Vermont, next door to the eighteenth-century converted sheep barn that was my house, next to an orchard and horse pasture. Tony Hawk I wasn't, but I wasn't about to give up trying. The ramp sat at the bottom of a steep and gravelly drive.

When skateboards reach a certain velocity, they begin to wobble back and forth. It's a terrifying sort of erosion of control, as the board begins a hyper-intense weaving back and forth as you try to keep your balance atop the plank of wood you've decided to balance on while rocketing down the hill. This is what happened, with my dubious father watching, when I chose to begin at the top of the steep hill on my first attempt at launching off our Pleistocene ramp.

That first attempt was an inglorious lesson in physics. I hit the base of the steep ramp, which at its zenith was probably a good four feet off the ground. The front wheels of my skateboard crunched easily into the particle board, bringing my board to an abrupt halt and flinging my body with a resounding slap against the ramp. Shaken but undeterred, my father and I covered the bottom part of the ramp with a sheet of aluminum that made the egress to the near-vertical height of the ramp a bit more manageable for the wheels of the board.

The next attempt was successful, depending on how you look at it. Skateboards then, some twenty-five years ago, still were miraculous in their construction. Swiss-engineered ball bearings were housed in dense, frictionless polymer wheels that spun with an incredible velocity and lack of drag. The speed I was going as I successfully hit the ramp was not recorded with any kind of technical equipment, so I have to rely on anecdotal reportage from my father, who was the only witness, and my own memory, which, due to the concussive result of said launch, is understandably a bit gauzy. I'm not saying there was an audible "pop" as a gawky adolescent broke the sound barrier at Dunham Orchards that day, but I'm not saying there wasn't.

I never got very good, but I loved the idea of it, and the way it seemed to make adults shake their heads in dismay and conjecture about the way in which *today's youth were wasting their time*. At that time, in the late 1980s, carrying your Santa Cruz or Powell and Peralta deck around was the closest you could get to flipping everyone the bird as you walked around town. To a disaffected teenager, it was manna from heaven.

I had to give it up as my work with kids moved into the wilderness. But for a few years in Los Angeles, I worked at a small elementary and middle school, and saw the opportunity to revisit my love of skinned knees and sprained wrists with my students.

I began a club, scheduled for Fridays after school, called Skate Club. It had, as its central focus, street skating, which is different from what we see nowadays in the Olympics. True street skating is exactly what it sounds like: taking to the streets and finding curbs and loading docks and parking lots to launch and grind and carve on. The kids and I would ride our boards around Pasadena, hitting up rails and curbs and hills and concrete riverbeds and anywhere we could find that presented an interesting place to ride. The kids named their Skate Club team "Team Freedom," which I thought fit nicely with the anarchistic underpinnings of skating. We'd carry chunks of wax in our cargo pants pockets to slick down curbs for grinding, buy *elote* from little carts pushed by Mexican vendors, and sometimes take the train into downtown Los Angeles and skate around Skid Row and Union Station.

Driving through any city now, I can still dial into the skater's perspective and see rails, curbs, stairs, and grinds. It's a secret topography, where the urban landscape is radically altered and becomes a playground, antithetical to its actual purpose, which is to grease the wheels of commerce. Skating is a very ironic enterprise in this way; urban cityscapes are designed with big business and adult concerns in mind. Grand edifices, concrete and steel and glass walls and walkways and plazas, all built with the thought that they will be used as physical accessories to the adult world of banking, commercialism, and bureaucracy. Skaters love these places: polished marble and grand, concrete staircases. They're perfect for skateboarding, which is, to borrow a term from the world of the gainfully employed, a net-loss enterprise.

We skated wherever it looked fun to skateboard, and were often shooed away by security guards. Skateboarding often incensed people who worked and used these places, and they'd come barreling out of revolving glass doors, spitting furious epithets, the razor burn over their Brooks Brothers collars turning scarlet with rage. I could never quite figure out what it was that made them so mad, but honestly, I think it might have been resentment over the freedom the kids exhibited. I think these bastions of commerce, these foot soldiers of the urban business world, hated the kids because they themselves were so far removed from what it meant to be a kid, to be careless and carefree, obnoxious and oblivious. We got chased away, and would always go, politely; that was the rule. Ask forgiveness not permission was our credo, and whenever we got yelled at we always left whatever spot we were skating, offering sincere apologies. The kids didn't sweat it. There was the entire city to skate.

But things didn't always go that smoothly.

It was a typical Friday, and we headed out after school to skate. We had decided to stay local. We rolled down the sidewalk, talking, laughing, and enjoying a typical Southern California afternoon. We headed into a neighborhood that abutted the street our school was on. It was a neighborhood that CalTrans had purchased with the hope of building a freeway; the freeway had never been built, so all these beautiful old homes were rentals, thus lowering the normally mortgage-based security-mindedness we found in more established neighborhoods. In other words, security was low and there were lots of places to skate.

We located a "gap," which is skater parlance for any space between two objects. The idea is to "ollie" the gap. Pop your board up and jump over the space. This one happened to be from one wide concrete wall to another.

We started taking turns trying to ollie the gap. Skateboarding is an exercise in failure. In order to do a trick successfully, skateboarders first must practice the trick, again and again and again, hundreds if not thousands of times. It is remarkable to see them trying to land some trick; they will literally attempt the same thing dozens of times, each time failing. But for some reason, unknown to me, there isn't the same level of frustration that you'd find in more traditional sports. The level of failure is an accepted piece of the culture; nailing a trick is great, but there is an equal amount of attention paid to eating it and getting shredded in epic bails.

Right before we finished skating the gap and headed off down the sidewalk, two things happened. First, I saw the silhouette of a woman in the home nearest to us. I had knocked on the door earlier, out of what I felt was an example of common courtesy I hoped to demonstrate to my young charges, and had not received a response from within. Whenever possible, I would try to ask permission of people to skate near, or on, their property. This set me apart from a lot of skaters, I knew, but I felt it was my job to bridge the gap between a criminal enterprise and urban education. Skateboarders are often seen as a public nuisance and riffraff; most major municipalities across the United States have invested thousands of dollars in "no skateboarding" signage, and many commercial entities have put "skate-stoppers" on particularly attractive ledges and rails to keep kids from grinding and boardsliding on their properties. I felt like I was a diplomat from the other side, a teacher, no less, reaching out to dispel the negative myth that surrounds skate rats.

A few minutes after I saw this silhouette of the woman, who appeared to be looking at us through a gauzy cotton curtain and talking on the phone, the second thing occurred—two police cars zoomed past us on the street. We were in a small parking lot abutting an apartment building. I quickly put two and two together.

"Let's go, guys," I said.

The boys had seen the police as well, and since we were, at this stage, familiar with what most authorities felt about our after-school activities, we quickly got on our boards and began moving back down the street. We were headed toward where my car was parked, near the school a block or so away, when a cop car, lights flashing and siren blaring, roared up beside us and screeched to a halt on the curb. The cop leapt from the car yelling.

"Off the board, now!" he said. We all slowed and stopped. A second car came careening around the corner, the lights on top flashing red and blue, and siren howling. It pulled in at the curb just like in the movies, with a sort of shuddering halt that left it nosed in at the curb right at us, as though the Chevy Caprice was hungry and if it wasn't for the curb would've jumped straight at our throats.

"Whoa, hey, guys, settle. It's alright, s'okay. I'm a teacher," I said, walking toward the closest cop, a blocky guy with a brutal crew cut, dark shades, and bowlegs. I held my hands out in a gentle gesture of slow down, back off. The cop snatched my wrist and whipped me around, jerking my arm behind my back.

"Hey!?" I was in shock. The kids were gape-mouthed and staring. The recently arrived cop car was now ejecting police like a clown car, and they were bearing down on my scraggly looking students, who stood like deer in the headlights.

"On the curb! Now!" the officer yelled. He zip-tied my wrists. He manhandled me to the curb and yanked me down onto my knees. This all happened in seconds.

"Officer, you have the wrong people here. I'm a teacher. These are my students. We're an after-school club. Take it easy!" My voice sounded unnaturally shrill and high. I felt electrified with fear, and was shaking in terror.

I was trying to talk over my shoulder as I kneeled awkwardly by the curb. I could see one of the students, Jake, being cuffed as well, his face pale. He looked ready to vomit. The other kids were still just standing around, frozen. Another siren blared; this time it was a police motorcycle. It was like we were on an episode of *Cops*.

The officer behind me moved away, and another (the third) cop car pulled up. This was getting ridiculous. I stood up, with no small amount of difficulty, and turned to address the nearest police officer, a severe-looking woman who stood behind me in a short-sleeved police uniform, her hair pulled back tightly in a glossy bun.

"Officer, these are my students. I'm a teacher. I can take you to our school . . . its right down the street."

I felt, somehow, in the dim, distant part of my brain not taken over by panic and fear, that if I could get the cops to take us to the school, maybe show them the classroom, that sort of thing, I could convince them that we were not, contrary to appearances, a group of derelict drug-addict skateboarders. We were a class out for an after-school club, for god's sake, which must be at least one level above crack dealers.

The woman wheeled, nostrils flaring.

"Down! On the curb!" she yelled, and her hand went to the butt of the gun holstered at her waist. I kid you not.

"Okay, whoa!" I said. I backed away and returned to the curb. By now all the kids were cuffed and seated twenty feet away on the curb, an officer taking down their names. They were on the edge of tears; some were already crying. The short, crew-cut officer came back over to me.

"ID?" he said. I didn't have any, and told him so. I didn't bring my wallet with me skating; it was bulky, and I was always afraid I'd lose it. This did not make him happy. He had patted me down when he sat me on the curb. He had taken my car keys.

"Which car is yours?" he asked. I nodded up the street to where the old girl sat. My stepmother had generously donated a mid-1980s Ford Crown Victoria to the Erik transportation initiative years before. It was dented and missing hubcaps and pretty dusty. If I was working on a Hollywood set and needed a car as a prop to build a scene involving down-and-out criminals, my Crown Vic would've been on a short list of choices.

Despite my love of the outdoors, of camping and rock climbing, and even though I tended toward activities like skateboarding and trespassing, I was also teaching students in the classroom at the time. In fact, I was working on a language arts project with some of the girls in middle school. One of them had expressed an interest in *Hamlet*, so we were filming little sections of the play as a movie. We'd pick locations throughout Pasadena, and film at night, with the kids doing scenes. I'd film with an old VHS camcorder, and we hoped that we'd be able to string together an hour of the play at some point.

The point of all this is that in the back of my car, the officers found a camera and various stage clothes including bodices for Ophelia, big, frilly Victorian dresses, and tights for Hamlet.

The cop with the crew cut surveyed the contents of my trunk, and looked back up at me. He'd taken off his wraparound shades at this point and stared daggers at me, no doubt thinking that he'd just nabbed a child pornographer.

There we were, me with no ID, with a pack of dirty, homeless-looking kids in tow, with a car full of fetish clothes and a video camera. They were not pleased with me, and shot me the kind of looks I imagine inmates did to Jeffrey Dahmer right before they stove his head in with a detached toilet lid in prison.

They loaded us in the cars. The backs of cop cars have plastic seats, and they don't give you seatbelts. It's basically a little bench. Our hands were tied behind our backs, making sitting in the car difficult. I was in a car with a student named Daniel, who seemed the least perturbed out of all of us.

"There goes Jake!" Daniel said as one of the other police cars passed us, and we saw the pale, terror-stricken face of Jake in the window. "Dude, let's wave!" Daniel said. He looked down at his arms, which, like mine, were still tied behind his back. "Oh, I forgot. I can't," he said, bemused.

We got to the police station and the cops unloaded Daniel from my car. They took him in a separate door. I complained, saying I needed to stay with my students, they were my responsibility. As one of the cops pulled Daniel from the car, I tried, even though I was scared shitless at this point—scared we were going to jail, that I'd lose my job, that the kids' parents would kill me, that I was going to have to learn to handle love "prison style"—to assuage what I assumed must be fears on Daniel's part.

"Daniel, it'll be okay. I'll get ahold of your parents. I'll come get you guys."

Daniel looked back at me, hands locked behind his back as the policeman maneuvered him out of the car toward a side door in the towering police station.

"Dude, we'll be alright," he said. He was smiling, and I realized in a groundswell of amazement that Daniel was having a good time. He was enjoying himself, the spectacle, the rush of danger. Teenagers. Gotta love 'em.

I, on the other hand, was not enjoying myself. I felt terribly guilty for creating this situation. The cop drove me down into the sally port where they disembarked dangerous criminals, like middle school teachers who skateboard with their students. The female officer led me through horribly windowless and bright corridors to a little room, where I was seated on a hard bench bolted to the wall. There was a small table on the other side, with a wheeled stool. The short male cop came in and switched with the lady. He brought with him a series of papers and forms, all on a big clipboard. He made a move to sit down on the stool, but due to his enormous gun belt and jack boots, and the smallness and close proximity of the room, he kicked the stool a bit with his heel and came down with just part of one ass-cheek on the edge of the black vinyl stool. It wasn't enough to hold him, and the stool simultaneously slipped and wheeled out from under him, and he fell awkwardly down on his ass. The clipboard clattered to the floor and papers flew. I rose out of instinct to help, the way, I think, anyone does when someone near them tumbles. It was just a little half rise off the bench, and I had to incline my upper body to propel myself up, as I was still cuffed and couldn't lift myself with my arms. I guess I moved too quickly, or maybe my bent-forward posture suggested I was going to try to launch a flying head-butt. The policeman, on his ass with legs sprawled on the floor, held one hand out at me to defend himself and the other grabbed at the butt of his pistol.

"No!" he shouted. I froze, and then quickly lowered myself back down. He scrambled up, cursing, gathering papers. His face was flushed crimson, and he wouldn't make eye contact with me.

"You okay, sir?" I asked. He didn't answer.

It was sort of awkward after that. I was fingerprinted, and they took mugshots. I was asked my name and other information a couple of times. I tried, several times, to re-explain the situation, but I got the poker face every time.

The cop led me up some stairs to the holding cells. The cells were all situated around a central station where the jailors sat. The jailors on this Friday afternoon were two guys who were watching an NBA playoff game on TV. The Lakers were winning. This was during the heady Shaq-and-Kobe dominance days. I was led, unceremoniously, to a little holding cell that was not meant for anything other than detoxification. It had a hard, narrow, concrete bench jutting out from the cinderblock walls and a lidless, stainless steel toilet. They took my belt and shoelaces from me before putting me in the cell, leaving me with big, floppy-tongue skate shoes and sagging pants that I had to hold up by clutching a section of bunched-up waistband in my fist.

I sat there in the cell, numb and stupefied. Had this actually happened? Had I just gotten my students and myself arrested for trespassing? What was happening to them? Were they okay? The only other inmate was a skeletal man in one of the other cells who was curled in the fetal position on the floor, head unhygienically close to the toilet, in my opinion. He looked to be in some stage of withdrawal, curling in on his need in an effort to extinguish the spark of it. His skin was ashen. I could smell him from where I sat.

The guards were talking with someone else in the station over a radio. I could hear snippets of the conversation.

"*. . . you got him in there yet?*"

"Yeah, we got him. He's in cell six."

"*. . . a teacher. We got his kids down in juvenile holding.*"

"No shit!"

"For real."

"Aw, man, he's a teacher? What you guys doin' with the kids? They scared?"

"... called their parents ... skateboarding on private property."

"No way, man! Oh shit!"

The two jailors—both of whom were African American—were laughing, and I could hear the voices on the other end laughing too. Apparently everyone thought it was a regular riot that I had been arrested with my students skateboarding on private property.

As I stood holding up my pants with my flopping shoe tongues dangling askew, I felt pretty pathetic and not very amused at all. I felt like I was about to lose my job.

The younger of the two jailors turned to me, eyes flashing with laughter.

"You got arrested on a field trip, man?" and he burst into more laughter.

I smiled. What else could I do? I sat down on the little bench bolted to the wall. It was so narrow you had to sit straight up, and I rested my head against the wall. Then I started thinking about vomiting crack addicts, and bloody criminals, and angry inmates peeing all over the place. I hastily stood up again.

The guards went back to watching the game. Minutes passed, then an hour. The guy in the next-door cell didn't stir, but new odors were highly suggestive of a functioning, if ill-timed, digestive system.

Finally, in the face of imminent termination, possible lawsuits, and incarceration, something happened. I grew bored. You can only be angry or stressed or scared for so long. Those are evolutionary emotions, designed to sustain a chase by a lion for as long as it takes us to get away. They're not designed to carry us through the ordeal of the modern criminal justice system.

"Can you guys turn the TV a bit so I can watch the game?" It was maddening listening to the commentators describe Kobe and Shaq and the rest of the team as they battled for West Coast dominance in the playoffs and not be able to watch. The guard smiled, and turned the TV. I situated myself in a way where I could stare sidelong through the yellow bars and see the screen, and the guards and I watched most of the second half together.

Looking back on the experience now, I realize that much of what happened to me was mitigated by the fact I was white. While my students were a regular Benetton ad—Korean and Black and Southeast Asian—I was white, and therefore was treated as a white person. If I was Black things would've been much different. Maybe fatal. That's just the reality; my skin was a ticket to treatment a Black guy never would've received.

As the game came to a close, the radio crackled again, and instructions were given. The guards came over to my cell. One of them had keys. I figured I was either headed to the big house in downtown Los Angeles, the city jail, where I'd likely pledge my undying love to some huge dude named "Bubba" and be rubbing his shoulders with Tiger Balm and giving him the choicest portions of my sloppy joe by morning, or I was going to be let go. I saw the second jailor had my shoelaces and belt. I felt tears well up in gratitude.

They let me go. The way they let you out of jail, when you haven't been officially booked, or cited, for anything, is pretty anticlimactic. They showed me to this door that opened up on a side street behind the station. It was dusk, when the smog of Los Angeles turns the sky a violent, bloody red. They shut the metal door behind me, and I heard the lock clunk home. There I was, in my floppy shoes, belt and laces in hand.

I took my shoes off and ran around to the front of the building. I didn't bother taking the time to re-lace my shoes or put on my belt; I just shuffled along as fast as possible. I knew I had to get to the front of the building and check on the kids. Where were they?

As I rounded the corner, I was met by all the boys from Skate Club. They'd been released and were standing there with their parents. I can't imagine what they thought when they saw me, shoeless, holding my pants up, covered in street grime from skateboarding. The look on my face must have been one of abject terror, because a few of them actually looked sorry for me. Most looked disappointed, and a few displayed expressions notably more stony and cold.

I stuttered apologies, swinging madly from abject, pathetic begging to desperate attempts at joking. It didn't go well. The parents started fading back, holding their boys protectively around the shoulders. The boys looked chagrined, and none of them really looked at me. I saw a few smirks, but mostly they looked pained at the ordeal they understood I was going through. I think a few of them were rightly concerned for their own hides, as well. I imagine some of them were very validly concerned their parents were going to sue me. Or have me shot.

Leon was being led out by his parents. Leon was Korean, and his parents had been generous to a fault. Korean culture holds teachers in high regard, and they had invited me over to dinner countless times, even taken me out to their favorite restaurants in Korea Town. Doubtless this recent escapade made them question my integrity, if not my sanity. Leon inclined his head toward me as he was drawn away by the gravitational pull of his parents' disappointment and anger.

"Dude, I know we're all going to be in trouble. But seriously, that was the best field trip ever."

21

A Lamentable Affair

THE DOG BROKE THROUGH THE ICE IN FRONT OF ME. SHE WAS GONE IN an instant. One moment she was happily trotting along the frozen river in front of me, the next she crashed through, and the only thing I could see for a moment was the dark, jagged gash of water. Then she surfaced, her head slick with water, popping up like a cork and immediately pawing at the ice in panic. She couldn't get a grip, and began to whine desperately. I skated toward her, and as I got close I heard the cracking under me. I stopped, the dog still scrabbling at the edge of the ice. Remembering that in these types of situations you were supposed to distribute your weight, I lay down on my belly and began inching forward. "C'mere girl! C'mon!" When I was within reach I heard a cracking sound, and the section of ice I was on dipped under my weight, water spilling toward my face.

People who live in the northern parts of the world—think Scandinavia, Russia, Alaska, and Canada—have been forced over hundreds of years to come up with creative ways to keep themselves busy over endlessly long winters of bitter cold. So they invented all sorts of entertainment: hockey, ice-fishing, electing Sarah Palin to office. But folks from the Nordic countries of Europe really shine in this regard. One of the popular winter pastimes for Bjorn and Astrid and Greta is Nordic skating. It's simple enough. The practitioner puts on a pair of ice skates, grabs a pair of ski poles, finds a frozen river, and takes a long winding day trip across the frozen wasteland. Then goes home and has a nice hot, naked sauna and enjoys universal healthcare.

While I didn't have a sauna, I was bored one winter in Vermont and gave it a shot. I lived with my family in a farmhouse at the foot of Snake Mountain. From our porch we could see the Lemon Fair valley, a patchwork quilt of fields and forest and the river itself. The Lemon Fair was a muddy, shallow, slow-moving river that drained the corn and hay fields that stretched for miles in every direction. Local history suggests that the river got the ironically cheerful name from early settlers who had tried to cross the river only to find their wagons buried up to the axle in the muddy clay that blanketed the valley. Apparently, one of those early settlers called crossing the river a "lamentable affair" and the name stuck, but was probably changed by early boosters of immigration desirous of driving up the tax base.

I put on my thrift store skates and grabbed a pair of cross-country ski poles and headed out, bringing along our golden retriever, Tasha. The day was bitterly cold—there's always a span of a week or so in Vermont where the temperature drops to zero and below and stays there. But the sky was clear and sunny, and the ice windswept and smooth. So I skated off upriver, the dog happily running along the banks and river's edge, exploring the wrack and ruin of past floods in the form of frozen logjams.

For some reason we think it's a good idea to bring into our homes small carnivores with a penchant for rolling in dead carcasses, eating feces, then throwing up on the rug. These animals are commonly known as "pets." People often get them as surrogate children or to accessorize outfits. It's estimated that humans domesticated dogs as long as thirty thousand years ago. It's no surprise; dogs are excellent companions who aren't bothered in the least by flatulence or nose-picking, unlike other fussy individuals such as spouses and children. I've had a dog most of my life. I don't think it's hyperbole to say that my life would be drastically different—*I* would be drastically different—were it not for the dogs I've known. I don't think I would've committed a large part of every day to getting outside, exploring the world around me, were it not for little four-legged beasties who need to poop and pee all the time. And once I'm out there, hiking along a trail with a dog whose tail wags happily up ahead, beckoning and urging me to come and explore with them, I am reminded not only of our inherent connection to all living creatures but also of the things that matter: friendship, fresh air, movement. Were it not for dogs, there's a chance I'd have to be surgically removed from the couch as I tried to find the end of Netflix. Dogs remind us of who we really are and who we could be if we simply let go and learned to have a bit more fun once in a while. They keep us on our toes.

In fact, this reality was brought home to me last winter. My daughter, Vivien, moved back home after graduate school and brought with her Phoebe, a fifty-five-pound pit bull mix she'd adopted. Phoebe had the physique of Jackie Joyner-Kersee—all muscle and sinew and speed. Phoebe had recently had surgery on both knees but was healed up, so

Vivien and I took her out on a hike in the woods and fields near our home, an area of hemlock and maple forests interspersed by cornfields, wetlands, and suburban parks. We brought along Ruggles, our other dog. Ruggles—or, if one is being formal, Mr. Jackson Cornelius Ruggles Esquire & Co—is a rescue who looks like the offspring of a hyena and a dingo. He's a great off-leash trail dog, however, so he joyfully scampered along beside us as Viv and I crunched through the snow, Phoebe pulling on her leash and trying out her new knees.

"Should we try letting her off?" Vivien asked. We were far from any roads and houses, surrounded by acres and acres of woods and fields.

"Why not," I said. Vivien reached down and with an audible *click* undid the leash from Phoebe's collar.

I have never in my life seen a dog take off so fast. Like a sprinting puma, and without so much as a glance back, Phoebe shot off through the field. She reached the edge of the forest in mere seconds and disappeared into the trees.

Ruggles tore after her, trying as hard as he could to keep up. Vivien and I turned to look at each other, mouths hanging open, the realization slowly dawning on us that we now had a predicament on our hands. Moments after he disappeared into the trees, Ruggles's head popped back out, looking at us, an expression of concern on his face that seemed to say, *Well, aren't you going after her?*

I took off running. It's important to note here that it was morning, and I had just thrown a big jacket and goofy, red snow pants over my pajamas. I was wearing large, cumbersome winter boots. Dressed in this ensemble, I took off after the dogs, jacket flapping, boots thumping. Uncaffeinated and barely awake, I sprinted for all I was worth after the dogs and into the trees.

It's at moments such as this I like to imagine I can see the scene from a bird's-eye view. Vivien, standing alone in the field, the now useless leash dangling from her hand; me, galumphing and wheezing after the dogs in my ridiculous winter getup; the dogs, running pellmell through the forest with tongues hanging out. *I am an adult with a job and a mortgage,* I thought as I heaved my recalcitrant body through the trees. *I don't need this.*

I caught up with them, eventually, as they'd found some interesting pee to sniff or dead things to roll in. But it was a great example of how dogs force you into an immediate and uncompromising engagement with the world. How your own selfish concerns about a promotion at work, the size and flubberiness of your love handles, or whether or not you drive a late-model sports car are superseded by the needs of a furry beast. They are four-legged harbingers of humility.

When Tasha went through the ice and I found myself in the draft of a Jack London story, I thought I might have lost her. I was worried that the current might be strong and drag her under the ice away from the hole she'd fallen through. I could just picture her sucked away by the dark waters, scratching away at the ice overhead. The ice was breaking in big, queen bed–sized pieces. The one I was on tilted toward the dog, and water poured over it, soaking my outstretched arms. Tasha still frenetically was trying to crawl up, but her paws couldn't get a purchase on the ice, and she had no leverage with her back legs, which were madly paddling beneath the surface to keep her afloat. I inched forward, pushing down the slab of ice and inviting more water to slosh toward me. Tasha had stopped whining and was now solely concentrated on survival, her brain shutting off all unnecessary functions and putting all resources toward hauling herself out of the freezing river.

Inching forward, I finally was able to grab her collar and haul backward. There was a moment where I thought the ice would give and dump me in too, and wearing a few layers of winter clothes I knew that I'd be in trouble, dragged down by their weight. Also, while I had never tried to tread water wearing hockey skates, I was pretty sure it wasn't a particularly efficient way to stay alive.

Inching backward in tiny increments, I was able to pull her front half out. Once she had more of her weight on the ice, Tasha was able to scramble up and out of the broken hole, now sloshing with chunks of ice that bobbed about. Staying on all fours, I scrabbled toward the bank behind the dog, who was making a beeline for solid ground. The adrenaline began to wear off, and I felt just how cold my arms and chest were, the icy water that had soaked through my clothes hitting me like an electric shock. I got to the bank and stood up, teetering on the blades of my skates as

Tasha furiously shook herself nearby. I took stock of the situation. I was a few miles from home, on a subzero day, and I was pretty wet—my hands already felt completely numb. I couldn't really walk anywhere, as I was wearing skates. Tasha was wet through and through, and the freezing air had already begun to suck our body heat away.

I took off my gloves and shoved them in a jacket pocket. Tucking my ski poles under my arm, I stuffed my frozen hands inside my jacket and buried them in my armpits. I began to slowly skate back the way I'd come, worrying that the ice would break under me any second. Tasha suspiciously eyed me from shore, but dutifully followed, keeping to the grassy frozen hummocks that lined the bank as we made our way back.

It is possible, I suppose, to have a lovely hungover Saturday morning where you stay in bed an extra hour instead of taking the dog out for spin. You can live a life where you don't have to consider the needs of your canine friend, whose beseeching eyes remind you constantly that it'd probably be a good idea to head outside for some fetch. I think it'd be fine to come home to a nice quiet house at the end of a long day and not be greeted by joyous insistence, wagging tails, barks, and full bladders needing release.

But why would you want that?

22

46ers

ANYONE WHO HAS HIKED THE HIGH PEAKS OF THE ADIRONDACKS knows that the trails were designed by demented trolls. Rather than take the landscape into account—say by using the tried and true method of switchbacks on steep inclines, as one does with other pathways such as wheelchair ramps and highways to ease the climb—the trails in the Adirondacks ascend every peak straight up, leaving hikers scrambling up shipping container–sized boulders and clinging to vertical water-slicked slabs while tiny flies feast on the sweat and tears pouring forth. Ironically, people actually go on vacation there.

My personal theory is that the trails of the High Peaks wilderness were designed to discourage visitors, thereby forcing all potential home-steaders downstate. That is why, my theory goes, New York City was invented, as a place to house some ten million frustrated hikers who gave up trying to enjoy themselves in the Adirondacks and settled instead for a scrubby island at the mouth of the Hudson full of pizza by the slice, street pretzels, and stockbrokers.

But camping is cheap, so I take my son, Finn, when we have the time. While some folks spend thousands on top-notch gear such as ultra-light tents, Vibram-soled boots, and wicking undergarments designed by NASA, Finn and I head out with stuff cobbled together from the basement and closets and strapped to our backs haphazardly, making us resemble some miner from the Klondike gold rush, clanging and totter-ing up the trail. My sleeping bag dates back to before the Kennedy era (I think it's stuffed with dodo feathers), and we both have foam sleep-ing mats that are laughably thin and ineffective. My camp stove weighs roughly one hundred pounds, and given my skinflint nature I cobble together meals from stuff I can find in our cabinets, so basically we eat pasta three times a day.

Over the years we've been trying to bag as many of the "46er" peaks as possible. There are forty-six peaks in the Adirondacks that are over 4,000 feet, and this exclusive club of 46ers is populated by hikers who, either through sheer obstinacy or a deep-seated self-loathing, have summited every single one. There is even a more exclusive clique within the 46ers, those who have summited each peak during the winter, always distinguishable by the fact that most are missing multiple fingers and toes due to frostbite and spend mealtimes stumbling about and dropping silverware. Finn and I have climbed twelve so far.

Now, many reading this account may be scoffing right now. Harumphing, even, as they read about tiny little peaks only 4,000 feet high. After all, Everest is 29,032 feet, and peaks in the Rockies and the Sierras are often over 14,000 feet. However, I submit to you that there are few trails as unenjoyable as those in the Adirondacks and, by extension, the Green Mountains in my home state of Vermont, just across Lake Champlain. It is not unusual to ascend nearly 3,000 vertical feet during one of these hikes on trails that forgo any semblance of decency and respect for knees that are forty-plus years old. In addition, hiking out west in places like Colorado and California, the outdoorsperson is rewarded constantly by Instagrammable vistas: soaring mountain ridges, sharp peaks, blue skies, and attractive, tanned people. Hiking in the East, however, especially in the Adirondacks, there is nothing to see but the muddy, boulder-strewn trail at your feet as you heave your carcass up what basically amounts to vertical stairs in a dense tunnel of overhanging trees that block out all light and hope, and people who are angry, sweaty, and fly-bitten. As families grumpily pass by, you can hear snippets of conversation between couples: *I wanted to go to Old Orchard Beach in Maine by the ocean but noooo, you had to bring us here.* What I am saying, in a nutshell, is that yes, the mountains aren't the tallest, but they are by far the cruelest.

Finn and I arrived at the parking lot for Rooster's Comb—not a proper peak but a nice vista—and prepared our gear for a few days out in the High Peaks region. We planned on summiting a half dozen of the 46ers over three days, and our packs were stuffed and heavy. The trail began in a swampy little lowland, hugging the shore of a muddy pond, but soon enough began to climb upward. The vegetation changed from the more-leafy, deciduous type of forest to piney woods pretty quickly. The weather was hot but overcast, the perfect environment for blackflies and mosquitoes, both of which attended to us as we shuffled our way up the trail.

I sweat. A lot. Not just a bead or two of perspiration on my upper lip, but gouts of sweat pouring down my body. I sweat during all activities, regardless of exertion level: ice-skating, bike-riding, dog-walking, filing taxes. My shirt was instantly sopping wet, particularly my back, where my pack was pressed, denying any air circulation at all. The few other hikers we passed stared at me the way you stare at a fellow diner at a restaurant who begins choking loudly on a dinner roll. Their very expressions seemed to ask, *Is medical intervention necessary? This man looks ill.* Finn took me in at a glance, and his thirteen-year-old expression was one of horror and disgust. "Dad, you're really sweaty," he said. "Yeah," I wheezed, wiping a pint of sweat from my face. "A bit."

The trail continued upward. We tramped gamely along, our pace slow and measured. Looking at the map earlier, I had planned a route that would take us over two of the 46ers: Lower Wolfjaw and Upper Wolfjaw. I realized, however, that it was unlikely we'd make it that far. Our pace was maybe a mile an hour, burdened by our packs and chugging along in the soupy heat. Finn seemed fine, the resilience of youth both a wonder and a source of deep resentment to those of use with gray hair; and Ruggles, our dog, bounded happily along, scouting the trail for us and finding many disgusting features of the landscape to roll in or eat.

We struggled on, but as the afternoon headed toward evening we figured we were nowhere near our goal. We broke off the trail, which snaked along the torturous ridgeline we'd followed all day, and headed down a valley to a lean-to for the night. After rinsing off in a river nearby, we prepared a meal of pure gluten and carbohydrates, eating in total silence and concentration, our mouths slurping the food while our eyelids drooped. We had brought little chlorinated tablets to treat our drinking water, but they gave the water a distinctly hot-tubesque flavor. So I boiled a large pot of water and filled our bottles, leaving the caps loosely screwed on to let the heat dissipate overnight.

Sleep came hard and fast, and despite the fact that the hard wooden floor of the lean-to was the antithesis of comfort, we both fell into a deep sleep almost immediately. Exhaustion is a wonderful sleep aid.

After rising in the morning and devouring chocolate chip pancakes, we slowly began packing up our gear. I had been so tired when I got into camp the night before, I had strewn my stuff everywhere—sweat-stained shorts hung from the rafters of the lean-to, and muddy sneakers were cast off in every direction. We gathered our gear and reluctantly stuffed our backpacks, preparing for the full day ahead of us. We hoped to summit Upper Wolfjaw, Armstrong Mountain, and Gothics, three more of the 46ers, before heading down to camp at another lean-to.

Once my lopsided and unwieldy pack was ready, I hoisted it onto my aching shoulders. Grabbing my water bottle, I took a big swig to pre-hydrate for the climb out of the valley back up onto the ridge. The water was still practically boiling. Apparently the heat had not escaped over the course of the night. There may be no greater misery than a hot hike during which, whenever thirsty, you have to slug down hot water. Unfortunately, due to the insulation properties of my water bottle, that's what I ended up experiencing all day, which meant that I dreaded every break we would take, as I had to swallow gulps of water that resembled nothing so much as hot spit. Finn had poured his boiled water out and replaced it with chlorinated water, and came up with a strategy of sucking an Altoid as he drank to mask the taste.

We climbed up out of the valley back up to the ridge, even this little effort taking well over an hour. Once we were back on the trail, we began climbing up and down unnamed humps and spurs along the route, each one a densely forested, rocky landscape of steep ups and downs. Whenever the trail dipped into a saddle between peaks and we had to scoot on our butts down sheer slabs of bedrock, the relief of finally going downhill was tinged with deep bitterness—every step down would eventually have to be regained on the next peak.

When we hit the climb up Armstrong Mountain, the first ascent was on a ladder built from thick, rough planks that had been bolted to the sheer face of a soaring wall of rock. I had to lift Ruggles in one arm and climb one-handed while carrying my pack, an enterprise roughly analogous to juggling on a unicycle while holding a colicky infant. The trail continued up Armstrong, massive blocks of gray stone the size of minivans interspersed with rooty, muddy catwalks, all piled on top of one another. In a way it could be fun scrambling up the trail, sort of like nature's playground. But with a pack on my back when I was already spent, it was tough. I'd lift my foot up and place it on the next ledge, located at waist height, grab overhanging roots and slender tree trunks, and with an intense, drawn-out grunt that sounded like I'd eaten a bowling ball and was now trying to expel it from my sphincter, I'd haul myself up a few feet. Finn and the dog would peer down from above, their expressions mirroring each other—one part concern, one part embarrassment.

It was at this point that I ran out of water, as did Finn. I had, in my deep reservoirs of unfounded confidence, figured that there would be little rivulets of water everywhere, happy burbling streams of clear, cold stuff we could refill with. This turned out not to be the case, however, for the simple reason that water, for those who aren't aware, is subject to gravity. Thus, when you're on a ridgeline and everything is, technically, *beneath* you on either side, there is no place from which the water can flow to get to you. Any moisture will flow downhill off the ridge. Despite the fact that this concept of physics is so rudimentary even Ruggles understands, it had not occurred to me. So we soldiered on, our saliva beginning to take on the consistency of saltwater taffy in our mouths.

There is one very long section in the *Lord of the Rings* trilogy by Tolkien where Strider, Legolas, and Gimli chase a band of hobbit-napping orcs across miles and miles of landscape. This part of the novel goes on and on and, for a book chock-full of action, is pretty boring on an objective level. But for anyone who's ever backpacked, especially in a place like the Adirondacks, there is such a feeling of empathy for the warriors of Middle Earth as they run, mile after mile, day after day, across Rohan. The very act of reading it mirrors the experience of the characters, drudgery in motion. As their legs persevere across endless hills and plains, the reader's eyes gobble up sentence after sentence like:

> *The sun climbed to the noon and then rode slowly down the sky. Light clouds came up out of the sea in the distant South and were blown away on the breeze. The sun sank. Shadows rose behind and reached out long arms from the East. Still the hunters held on.*

And then:

So the third day of their pursuit began. During all its long hours of cloud and fitful sun they hardly paused, now striding, now running, as if no weariness could quench the fire that burned them. They seldom spoke. Over the wide solitude they passed and their elven-cloaks faded against the background of the grey-green fields; even in the cool sunlight of mid-day few but elvish eyes would have marked them. Until they were close at hand.

And on and on:

The sun was sinking when at last they drew near to the end of the line of downs. For many hours they had marched without rest. They were going slowly now, and Gimli's back was bent . . . Aragorn walked behind him, grim and silent.

Bent backs, resentful silences—yep, sounds like a hike in the Adirondacks.

After summiting the Gothics we made our way down the steeply pitched rock slabs, clinging to huge cables someone had bolted to the rocks to assist in the descent. It was early evening, and the sky was clouding over even more darkly; rain looked possible. According to the map, it looked like about a mile down the valley there was a river and a lean-to. We were parched and exhausted, and the thought of fresh, cool water and a place to sleep nice and dry seemed almost erotically appealing.

Stumbling and quiet, we made our way down the slippery trail toward the river. Finally, after about an hour, we came to the first trickles of water, but they were choked with reddish effluent (some kind of mineral) and smelled like a rhino's ass. Despondent, we kept walking, our pack straps now feeling like iron bands wrapped over our shoulders. The light was fading and the air was changing; it was definitely going to rain.

Finally, we found a mossy little stream in a deep, shady gorge. We filled our bottles, dropped in the chlorine tablets, and waited the twenty minutes required to kill any bacteria or cute little squiggly-wigglies that might be residing in the water. Finn stretched out on his back on a flat slab of rock near the stream, and I stared mutely at the trickling water, checking my watch approximately every seven seconds.

That first sip—manna from heaven. We chugged and slurped, our desiccated bodies loudly demanding more. We both felt better almost immediately, and headed off down the trail, knowing we must be within spitting distance of the lean-to.

Finally, after more stumbling in the gloam of the forest, we heard voices. Lean-tos in the wilderness of the Adirondacks are first-come, first-served. Most have additional tents sites nearby in case of overflow, so we didn't worry much as we made our way toward the sound of folks camped at the lean-to.

The structure was just off the trail up a little hill in the thick trees. I headed up, Ruggles bounding happily ahead of me to meet whoever was camped there.

The lean-to was packed with teenage girls. They were all gabbing happily, looking clean and scrubbed, their packs neatly leaned up against the inner walls of the lean-to. They looked organized, as though they were in the middle of some sort of planning session, and one of the young women stood facing the group as though she'd been addressing them before I showed up.

Ruggles began spastically insinuating himself among them, whining and wagging and begging for pets without any pride whatsoever. I addressed myself to the woman who seemed to be in charge.

"Hi, how's it going? Is there a good place to get water here?"

"There's a river right down there," she said, gesturing over her shoulder.

We chatted; I learned it was an orientation trip for counselors at a Christian girl's camp. They did have that squeaky-clean, holier-than-thou sort of vibe, contrasted sharply by our own filthy, trail-muddied appearance. In any case, there were about a dozen of them, so it was pretty clear that the lean-to, at least, was full.

Finn and I extracted Ruggles from his undignified efforts to lick every face and went down to the river. We began filling our bottles and treating the water, and tried to figure out what to do.

"Should we stay here? I can ask them if there's any tent sites open," I said.

"Or we could just walk all the way back to the car," Finn said. This, while deeply appealing, was a near impossibility; we had at least six miles to the nearest road, and then several miles of walking the road until the car. It was almost dark; we'd be walking in pitch blackness. Still, I have to admit I considered it.

"Look, we're tired, and it looks like it's going to rain. Why don't we just grab a tent site, and we'll camp here for the night?"

Finn looked wan and hungry. He stared back up toward where the lean-to was hidden in the trees. "Okay," he said.

I left him there by the river and headed back up toward the lean-to to see what the story was with tent sites. I got to the base of the little hill and started up.

I was met with a disturbing sight. The troupe of Christian counselors-in-training had been told, clearly, that as cleanliness was next to godliness it was time to brush teeth. They were all scrubbing away, frothy foam erupting from the sides of their mouths. They were also slowly walking downhill, away from the lean-to. So as I approached, what I saw was a slow-marching army of shark-eyed Christian teenage girls foaming at the mouth heading straight for me.

"Oh my god, I'm sorry, didn't know I was interrupting tooth-brushing time," I said awkwardly, feeling a bit weird at barging in on what is usually a semi-private act. Also, I was fully aware that I was a forty-seven-year-old man, stinky and grimy, approaching a cluster of Christian teenage girls. Give me a machete and a hockey mask and we could've been cast in a horror movie.

I'm also aware of some subconscious sarcasm here. After all, I said, "Oh my god," which is taking the lord's name in vain. And on some level I did that on purpose. It just slipped out.

The weirdness of the moment was broken as Ruggles, ever eager to jump up, muddy-pawed, in someone's face, came wriggling and whining with tail wagging furiously up to one of the girls. She stared down with undisguised contempt at him.

"Ew. I don't *do* dogs."

Now, I get that. Not everyone is a fan. But the sheer disgust she demonstrated seemed a bit severe for the situation, I thought. I grabbed Ruggles's collar and pulled him away, and made eye contact with the young woman who seemed to be the mentor. I put on my nicest "I'm not a weirdo kidnapper" face and smiled brightly. "Is there a tent site that's open? I think we're just going to camp here tonight. Looks like rain."

Her face instantly set like stone into a severe countenance devoid of emotion. She didn't look angry, just hard. "There's no more sites. They're all full," she said.

There was an awkward pause; the girls around us stopped brushing and watched silently.

"Oh, okay. None?"

"All full."

I stood for a moment more, as about a thousand responses bubbled up. In the end I said nothing, just smiled and nodded, and headed back down the trail, feeling the stares of a dozen righteous Christians laser into my back. I squatted down next to Finn and told him there was no camping to be had. We were out of luck, and would have to walk down the trail and find somewhere else to camp. It was now twilight; the forest was growing dark.

We packed up and began picking our way through the gloom.

"Not very Christian of them, was it?" I said.

"What?" Finn asked.

And it was here that I launched into a furious diatribe about the hypocrisy of religion. It was the sort of fiery speech that will, no doubt, send Finn to therapy as an adult.

"I mean, I understand the impact the Judeo-Christian mindset has had on the world. I'm a professor, right? The whole point of the gospels, and the basic message of Jesus, is to help those in need, am I right? Well, we're kind of in need of a place to sleep. And those girls just wouldn't help. They just wouldn't! What kind of Christianity is that, huh? I'll tell you what kind. Greedy Christianity. Poseur Christianity. I mean, who do they think they are? I thought the whole Christian creed was to help those in need of charity. Well, look at us? Bug-bitten and tired, and they couldn't even offer us a wedge of ground to pitch a tent!"

It went on in this way for quite some time. I veered into a long discussion of how Christian greed manifested itself as the desire for eternal life in heaven, as if this life, this world, wasn't good enough for them, and I believe I may have compared the Christian desire for a second life of celestial joy in heaven to a grossly rich person buying a golden toilet because a regular toilet just wasn't good enough, a clunky metaphor that may have confused Finn into thinking that heaven was somehow related to plumbing and nouveau riche gaucheness.

Night was falling, and soon we were walking with only our head-lamps' beams illuminating our surroundings. Finn, poor guy, was tired, but I was still going on about the cyborg Christian girls who'd denied us a chance to camp. I was on a roll now, and couldn't be stopped. I was talking about how, obviously, there are decent Christians out there who did a lot of good. But many who were just full of themselves, postur-ing as pure and innocent souls when they were anything but. I then started regaling Finn with stories of Christian-run "Indian schools" in the United States and Canada, and how these institutions systemati-cally destroyed native culture, and often murdered children as well, as a means of stamping out Indigenous populations. How Christians were responsible for upholding the very idea of Indigenous genocide, and that Finn's ancestry—on his mom's side relatives came from Indigenous communities in the Sonoran Desert regions of Mexico—was subject to a crusade of wholesale cultural and actual slaughter by missionaries and a large-scale Christian ethos that plowed over Indigenous sovereignty and dignity.

"I know Dad, jeez," Finn said, as the light from our lamps illuminated skeletal tree trucks and slick rocks.

At this point, emotionally exhausted, dehydrated, and hypoxic, I really let it rip. I began telling Finn that, in fact, the story of Adam and Eve was really just a mythology-cloaked manual for an Indigenous pogrom. Adam and Eve—living in the garden of Eden, naked, unashamed, and happy—are the perfect substitutes metaphorically for Indigenous cultures. And of course, Adam and Eve got kicked out, punished, and replaced by Cain and Abel, murderous farmers.

"The whole thing was just an elaborate scheme to divest native peo-ples of land and autonomy, and what we just experienced is so indicative of the sort of false Christianity practiced by so many people, just a per-formative superiority over others that has no real grounding in empathy or sympathy. And just like missionaries and early settlers used Christian values to validate the theft of Indigenous lands, those Christian camp counselors used them to rob us of a place to sleep!"

Eventually, I tired myself out ranting against teenage Christian girls. We clomped onward in full darkness. After about an hour, we finally found another lean-to that was uninhabited by selfish zealots and got ready for bed.

In the morning, after a leisurely breakfast and packing up, we hiked out and back to the car. The day was hot and sunny, and when we finally made it back to our little parking lot, the act of pulling our packs off and hurling them into the back of the car was a pleasure so deep it nearly brought me to tears. Finn had the bloom of youth, so he still looked fresh and healthy—looked even brighter for all the fresh air and exercise— whereas I looked like I'd been living in the trenches of World War I for a month, eating rats and staving off gangrene. I smelled rancid, my body muddied and scratched.

We drove straight to a gas station, and walking into the air-conditioned splendor I was struck by the abundance of it all: Little Debbie snack cakes and Pop-Tarts and Pringles and every single soda you could ask for. Snickers and Reese's and Slim Jims and you name it. All under the shimmering fluorescent light, it was like a citadel built to worship at the feet of the god of corn syrup. I've always loved gas stations and convenience stores, especially on road trips. I think the American roadside gas station satisfies some primal foraging instinct we've hung onto since our days as hairy savannah dwellers. We scrounge up and down the aisles, tuning into our libidinous, calorie-hungry id, grabbing to-go meals we'd never eat at home. "Dinner tonight? Well, looks like I'll be having Cool Ranch Doritos, Reese's Peanut Butter Cups, a thirty-two-ounce cup of coffee that could take the paint off a barn, Sour Patch Kids, and a family-sized bag of jalapeño and cheddar sunflower seeds, all washed down with Strawberry Muscle Milk."

We loaded up our arms with donuts and Gatorades and potato chips, went back out to the car, and began stuffing our faces with junk food.

It had been a long trip—at least spiritually. I kept thinking about the Christian campers and how steamed they'd made me. Maybe I was being intolerant, I thought. Anti-religious. After all, they were entitled to their views and beliefs. And maybe my annoyance at them was driven simply by the smugness of their youth, the way they claimed both tent sites and their identities with such absolute surety. Like any time spent out in the wild, it already seemed like a long time ago. Only three days and two nights, but I felt we'd come so far. We'd seen so much, pushed ourselves to such extremes.

I tried to think of something to say. Some way to capture the experience in words, put a stamp on this moment in time when father and son are together, burn these minutes in Finn's memory before he grows up and leaves behind his youth, heads off to have his own adventures and independence. Say something that offers us both a hook to hang our collective memories on. Perhaps offer Finn, and myself, a few words to commemorate this time together, celebrate the bond of love that had borne us through the wilderness.

"Forgive, and you will be forgiven," I intoned.

"What?" he said through a mouthful of donut, looking at me suspiciously, picking up on the possible moral implications of what I was saying and immediately becoming wary of a lecture. He had a Gatorade in his fist and a bag of chips on his lap. He had looked dirty and happy, but now a quickly darting cloud of skepticism crossed his face.

"Never mind," I said. And began the long drive home.

23

The World's Largest Chopsticks

FOLKLORE IS FULL OF WATER SPIRITS. HARDLY SURPRISING; THERE'S just something about a secluded pool, deep in the forest, that gives rise to fantasies of mermaids and nymphs, satyrs and fairies. The obsession is prevalent in Greek mythology—Narcissus was cursed by his own reflection in a pool of water. Celtic folklore in particular relishes tales of the sopping wet variety. Look at the Arthurian legends. At their core, the whole cycle of myths about King Arthur, Excalibur, Guinevere, Lancelot, and Sir Gawain and the Green Knight—which sits at the core of British culture—is centered around a foundational story of a lake, and a lady who apparently lives there and hands out swords. The echo of these stories rebounds today, with Daniel Radcliffe stripping down to his skivvies and diving into a pool of water to fetch Godric Gryffindor's sword in the cinematic interpretation of J. K. Rowling's *Harry Potter* series. There's just something about water that compels the imagination.

I've spent my life spellbound by pools, waterfalls, and swimming holes deep in the forest. Instead of sylphs or elves, naiads or fairies looking to sucker me in to some eternally bonding curse, I usually find a few drunk rednecks chugging tall boys of Natty Light. And yet, if I squint past the beer guts and broken glass, I can still see the hazy outlines of magic in these watery spots.

I think we can all agree; the internet has been a disaster. But if there's anything redeeming about the net, it's the site swimmingholes.org. It's a user-generated site that lists good spots for a dip all over the country. I look at the site with the fevered secrecy of a fifteen-year-old watching porn.

In the late nineteenth century, British scholar Sir James George Frazer wrote the urtext on the subject of myth, *The Golden Bough*, an exhaustive comparison of myths from across the globe. Fancy-pants British guy has this to say about water spirits:

In many of the tales the monster, who is sometimes described as a serpent, inhabits the water of a sea, a lake, or a fountain.

The Oyampi Indians of French Guiana imagine that each water-
fall has a guardian in the shape of a monstrous snake, who lies hidden
under the eddy of the cascade, but has sometimes been seen to lift up its
huge head. To see it is fatal.

The perils of the sea, of floods, of rapid rivers, of deep pools and
lakes, naturally account for the belief that water-spirits are fickle and
dangerous beings, who need to be appeased by sacrifices. Sometimes
these sacrifices consist of animals, such as horses and bulls, but often the
victims are human beings.

There is a draw toward water in all of us. Whether the beach or a buggy, shady pool deep in a woodsy grove, we're inescapably drawn toward the wet places in the world. There must be some elemental urge to be near these places, a hardwired connection to these watery spots.

There are plenty of things about a proper swimming hole that can deter visitation. There's often trash, cast aside by inebriated revelers: a single flip-flop, shattered Corona bottles, cigarette butts, and Dorito bags. The detritus of the proletariat, eager to taste the respite and freedom that relaxation provides the one percenters, who scooch lower in their deck chairs at Club Med while some local inhabitant shackled by neocolonial economies whisks away their empty mimosa glasses.

A decent swimming hole is, by definition, hard to get to. Bush-whacking through the woods is often a prerequisite. Water is the breeding ground for the larval flukes of mosquitoes and other buzzing, biting insects, and it is not unusual to leave a good river spot with goiter-sized lumps all over, courtesy of vampiric flies.

The footing sucks. Slippery, ankle-spraining jumbles of inappropriately sized and placed rocks give way to slick, wet ledges of sharp-edged rock. The safety of rocky banks is, at best, a mirage; the mossy slickness is about as easy to navigate as a hockey rink on roller skates.

And the water. Dear reader, I do not know, fully and completely, what masochistic personality flaw compels me to swim in these rivers. The water at a good, hidden swimming hole is testicle-shatteringly frigid, birthed from the dark icy heart of the mountains. When leaping off the rocks to plunge into the darkness, breath is slammed out of the lungs by the sheer shock of freezing temperatures. Swimmers at a gorge in the woods jump into pools only to resurface instantly with a wide-eyed look of animal panic. Even the most graceful Olympic synchronized swimmer is reduced to a sputtering, gasping, flailing mess, arms and legs thrashing wildly as they desperately look for the closest place to escape the glacially frosty nightmare they've willingly entered. Moments after hitting the water, cold knifes its way in so deeply the body seems to lock up, limbs, torso, and internal organs succumbing rapidly to a frosty rigor mortis. Deliberate thought is replaced by an impenetrable wall of sheer numbing fear.

Then, as quickly as possible, an escape is enacted from the water. Clambering out, slicing knees and feet on sharp-edged rocks, the jumper considers doing it again, purple-lipped and shrieking.

There's never a comfortable place to sit—no sugar-sand beaches here—and inevitably I drop my towel and backpack stumbling across the river, and end up hunched, shivering amid the rocks, eating water-swollen Cheezits with numbed fingers.

One of my favorite swimming holes is Bingham Falls. Located in a small, woodsy, steep-sided gorge in the shadow of Mount Mansfield, Vermont's tallest peak, Bingham is the exemplar of the swimming hole aesthetic. A round, greenish pool is fed by a forty-foot cascade, the waterfall tumbling down mossy rocks and ledges.

In the film *Japanese Story* from 2003, starring Australian actress Toni Collette and Japanese heartthrob Gotaro Tsunashima, there's a scene in which Tsunashima's character, Hiromitsu, a Japanese businessman who is having an illicit affair with Collette's character, dives into a rocky pool of water deep in the Australian outback. He hits his head and dies. The movie is beautiful and tragic and evokes questions of longing and love, truth and consequences, but all I could think after watching was, *Who dives headfirst into a swimming hole without checking for rocks first?*

I have a friend who has a daughter who has to poop every time she goes swimming. The kid jumps into the water—river, pool, lake, or sea—and within moments looks back at her mother with an expression of impending shame, humorous aw-shucks vexation, and mild impatience. And it's off to the nearest bushes or porta-potty. It's not unusual if you think about it. The water buoys us up, allowing the muscles and bones that prop us against gravity's pull to relax, and the gentle weight of water pressure massages us from all sides. It's a miracle, really, that every public pool isn't a toxic biohazard with schools of floating fecal Snickers bars bobbing in the surf.

A good swimming hole, with a waterfall and encircled by ferns, is a portal to another world. It's no wonder that waterfalls figure heavily in the imagination as thresholds to mystery. Michael Douglas and Kathleen Turner discover the emerald El Corazon behind a thundering cascade in 1984's *Romancing the Stone*. Mikey finds the treasures of the town wishing well behind a sheet of water in *Goonies*. Frodo and Sam palaver with Faramir at Henneth Annun, the respite hidden behind water falling into the Forbidden Pool in Tolkien's classic *The Lord of the Rings*. Grendel issues forth from some boggy sump, and Anglo-Saxon stud Beowulf dives deep into the same watery fen to kill the mead hall wrecker's lumpy mother.

The swimming hole, glade-encircled forest pool, contains mysteries unknown. Even in literature, the presence of the woodsy swimming hole elevates the narrative to the celestial and wondrous. In "The Forest Path to the Spring," Malcolm Lowry traces the wonder and magic, the geographic draw, of the hidden water source deep in the trees. I think. I've never been able to finish that essay.

But often bad things happen in secluded pools. When Han, Luke, Leia, and Chewie slosh around waist deep in grimy sludge while hiding in the trash compactor aboard the Death Star, what lurks in the water? An alien beastie known to Star Wars nerds as a dianoga, of course. But despite their reputation for harboring hungry monsters, we seek these places out. Because they are portals—gateways—to other worlds, we are drawn to them to escape the banality of the daily grind. Salvation and terror, bound up in one. Water is associated with purity and cleanliness as well as filth; there's no rat worse than a bilge rat.

I had taken a motley group of kids on an adventure to Bingham Falls. We'd hiked through the woods, kids slinging about lunch boxes and towels. Laughter scattered squirrels and birds as the crew made its way down a sloping, rocky trail. We could hear the falls before we even got there, catch glimpses of the white torrent through the trees.

The trail became steep and led us down a muddy incline to the base of the falls, where Volkswagen-sized boulders ringed a large pool at the base of the waterfall, and the water streamed and whirled downriver through a narrow, chute-like ravine. It was crowded with people eager to swim on a hot afternoon. I positioned myself where I could keep an eye on the kids, and they began exploring and jumping, shouting and shrieking and dunking in the cold water.

After a while, Nyah came swimming over to me. Her expression was tinged with panic.

"Erik, I have to go to the bathroom."

This wasn't unusual. Often, when taking kids on adventures in the woodsy parts of the world, I'd run into a young soul (or, frankly, older ones too) who'd never availed themselves of the magical opportunity afforded by swimming in lakes and rivers and oceans. The world becomes your toilet. Pee is basically water anyway.

"Just go in the water," I said.

"It's not pee."

Some internal mechanism in my chest ratcheted up a notch. This was not good. I'd been here before.

Bingham Falls had a healthy occupancy that day. Day-tripping locals looking to cool off, vacationing families taking the plunge amid the splendor of the overhanging hemlocks and maples. Folks were spread downriver a fair distance. The falls were in a narrow, steep-sided gorge.

"I have to poop," Nyah said.

"Okay, give me a min."

"Now."

There are those of us who can anticipate when the train may be arriving at the station. We check the schedule and determine the next likely arrival and make plans. But some—kids—don't want the exigencies of digestive machinations to interrupt a good time. Therefore, they ignore nature's gentle reminders until it's too late.

My father is a fly fisherman. I'm not sure why. Fly fishing is, for the uninitiated, the single most frustrating outdoor sport in the history of humanity. Any random Joe would have better luck taking down a mammoth with a slingshot than casting a weightless, hand-tied fly roughly the size of a molecule into a cold, dark pool resembling a teacup without getting their line inextricably tangled in an unhelpful protrusion of riverbank vegetation. What I remember from all the times Dad took me fly fishing is extreme, existential boredom; a persistent notion that I was being offered as some kind of all-inclusive human buffet for the biting insects of the world; and a dissertation-length internal monologue about how fantastically inaccurate the fishing scenes from *A River Runs Through It* are, Brad Pitt's rakish good looks notwithstanding.

Every dad wants to share his passions with his children. My dad wanted to give me the gift of fishing. On one occasion, he brought me down to the river behind our home in the mountains of Vermont where I grew up. I was about four. He began casting, which, for those lucky enough to have never fly fished, is akin to tying a few of your eyelashes in a small knot, attaching it to the end of fifty yards of dental floss, and then trying to whip your eyelash bundle across a foaming rapid into a pool of water the size of a toilet by lashing the line over your head. The line, by the way, is attached to a nine-foot length of recalcitrant and disobedient fiberglass that quivers and leaps about at the slightest touch like a coked-up dachshund.

Dad was casting about, pausing every few minutes to disentangle his line from some overhanging branches and provide me, through indirect instruction, with some choice new vocabulary I could show off on the playground. I toddled about flipping over stones, splashing in the water.

An important point here is that at this juncture in my young life I'd never caught a fish. Never tossed in my line, carefully drawing my fly through the water, to feel the powerful strike of a hungry trout, then a quick jerk to set the hook, and the artful play of angler vs. trout as I reeled in a beauty. No. I was just a kid. But my dad wanted to share his love of the sport with me, and so had brought me down to the Neshobe River with him.

As my dad fished and I wandered, whatever I had eaten for breakfast that morning made its way through my digestive system. In with the new, out with the old, as they say. I was caught short. There, on the banks of the Neshobe, I had to poop.

"Dad," I said.

"Hm," he replied, not looking at me. He can be laser-focused, my old man, when he's fishing. He stared hard at the spot in the river where he was casting, almost as though he hoped that the intensity of his gaze would will a sixteen-inch trout to appear, mouth wide and hungry.

"Dad, I have to go to the bathroom."

"Just go in the bushes," he said, still casting with metronomic efficiency, eyes locked on the river, hoping against hope that one of these casts would drop the fly in the right spot.

What my dad didn't realize was that the bathroom situation was a number two, not a number one. However, given my age and the lack of development in my prefrontal cortex, I took him at his word. I trundled over to some bushes next to the river, dropped my pants, and commenced the act of evacuating my bowels.

It was at this moment that a trout hit my dad's fly with a sudden splash. My dad, eyes wide as a gambler whose horse overtakes the lead in the final stretch, frenetically started alternately reeling in line and feeding out slack as his pole arced and bent wildly.

"Erik!" he shouted, still not looking, eyes on the prize. "Erik! Come on!"

I think in retrospect what he wanted was a sort of Norman Rockwell-esque scene: He'd hand me the rod, steady my young frame in his arms, and patiently guide me in landing the fish. Bonding moment supreme.

However, I was squatted over my freshly dropped turds. But, like many kids, I was a literalist and eager to please my father. Excited, too, at the prospect of a fish! So, without pulling up my pants, or paying heed to where I stepped, I bolted toward my father, anticipation thrumming my body like a plucked string.

My father remembers it thus: He turned, while playing the trout, to see where I was. He saw me scurrying over the rocks toward him, pants around my ankles, naked nethers a-dangle. As I drew close, my dad caught the reek of fresh excrement, and a cursory glance confirmed it. I'd stepped in my own poop, and my shoes were covered. Desperate to take part in this sportsman's rite of passage, I'd run the gauntlet of my own feces to be there with my dad at our moment of triumph.

Nyah began to scramble out of the water, a panicked seven-year-old in a two-piece swimsuit. She was rapidly swiveling her head back and forth, looking for a suitable spot, I assume, to drop her bottoms and commence the deed. We were surrounded by at least two dozen other swimmers.

"Nyah, not here!"

"I have to go!"

I grabbed her hand and hurriedly began leading her over the awkwardly jumbled boulders of the riverbed. We had at least one hundred yards to go downriver before the steep banks mellowed and would allow us a chance to get into obscuring foliage.

We slipped and scurried over the rocks, the cacophony of happy, shrieking swimmers and the merry splashing thunder of the falls echoing around us.

"It's coming!"

I don't know if I've ever heard a child's voice so plaintive yet tinged with terror. It almost matched the extreme level of fear I myself was experiencing. The way she said "it's coming" was with the same tenor and timbre one would announce a tornado or tsunami. Clearly, whatever "it" was, was a thing to be abjectly feared.

Frightened, I desperately looked for a spot for her to relieve herself out of public view. She was trying to drop into a crouch as we stumbled along, me pulling her through people and wet rocks, forced downriver by the vertiginous cliffs on either side like bovines in a cattle chute being led to slaughter.

From the corner of my eye, I saw it. A sparse series of hand- and footholds, more stone-age ladder than path, climbed the wall to my left. After about twelve feet, it looked as though there was a ridiculously narrow goat path etched in the rock, leading upward. It was our only hope.

Nyah had started to emit a high-pitched animal whine. I hauled her behind me as I scaled the wet, pine needle–strewn face. Somehow, most likely by dint of sheer adrenaline-fed survival instinct, we made it up to the goat path. We were now up above the heads of the swimmers, some of whom had by this point turned and watched as our scurrying dash attracted attention.

With a guttural cry Nyah ripped her hand from mine, whipped down her bathing suit bottoms, and within a second was disengaging a turd the size and girth of a midsummer zucchini.

She was clinging to the cliff side, awkwardly squatting on the impossibly narrow ledge-like path that veered sharply upward. I turned back toward the swimming hole and fully realized my folly.

We were perched on display, in full view of the dozens of folks below, like some vulgar Paleolithic cave painting come to life. Fingers pointed, jaws dropped.

To her credit, Nyah discharged her duty with aplomb and efficency. Once she'd dropped her prize, she hitched up her bathing suit bottoms, the look of relief clear on her face. She glanced from me to the poop, then back to me with an open, guileless expression.

"Go rinse off," I said.

Disaster averted (from her point of view), Nyah gamely climbed back down into the throng of swimmers to wash in the river. I stayed on the narrow shelf of rock, casting furtive glances at all the onlookers who continued to watch my predicament, the way it'd be hard to look away from a slow-motion car crash.

Nyah's excrement lay in full view. The unspoken demand of those watching, as well as some deep but undeniable moral principle, demanded what must be done. And yet I lacked the courage.

But the poop would have to be moved.

One cannot be responsible for leaving a fresh turd in full view of a beautiful spot like Bingham Falls. It would be an egregious sin, blasphemy in the extreme. And yet, clad in only swim trunks with no equipment, I was at a loss as to how to remove the offending item. I certainly was not going to pick it up with my bare hands.

My eyes skittered about, looking for something. Anything. A solution. I felt, rather than saw, the tension growing in the spectators below. The poop gleamed dully in the sun. I saw, farther up the goat path, a smashed and broken dead pine tree, hanging down the steep-sided wall, its roots still tenuously holding fast to the top of the cliff. Branches stuck out at odd angles. I knew what I had to do.

I scrambled up the rock and snapped off two branches, each as long as my arm. I edged back down to the scene of the crime, noticing in my peripheral vision the upturned faces of the swimming hole revelers now almost universally held in sway by the dramatic scene unfolding above their heads.

With the precision of an atomic physicist handling plutonium, I used my makeshift pinchers to carefully lift up the poop, holding it away from my body. It was impressively turgid and—luckily for me—had enough structural integrity to hold together. With sweat beading my brow, I gingerly made my way up the narrow path. My focus was a thing of steel. I was able to make it up to the zenith of the path where the trees and foliage provided welcome cover, and where I could finally dispose of Nyah's gift. With a strength and fury that suddenly and inexplicably rose within me, I buried it under a massive pile of dirt, rocks, and organic detritus I ripped barehanded from the earth.

Stepping away, I took some deep breaths. The sounds of kids playing in the river below echoed off the rock walls. I thought of Frazer's *Golden Bough*: "The Oyampi Indians of French Guiana imagine that each waterfall has a guardian in the shape of a monstrous snake, who lies hidden under the eddy of the cascade, but has sometimes been seen to lift up its huge head. To see it is fatal."

Indeed.

24

Waffles in the Afterlife

The world does not deliver meaning to you. You have to make it meaningful.

—ZADIE SMITH

NOT EVERY OUTDOOR ADVENTURE HAS TO BE EXOTIC. SOMETIMES I'LL just head out into the suburban/industrial wastelands around our home. Medical offices, auto repair shops, a FedEx distribution center. But near those rectangular monstrosities is a wedge of dark pine forest. A swampy, cattail-choked seep. Waving fields of goldenrod.

One day, Finn and I headed out to explore the waterfront of the lake near where we live. Formerly an industrial waterfront, now it sports a bike path and scrubby woods. Its history as a shipping port remains in the name of the strip of sand nearby, however: Texaco Beach.

We walked through the waterfront park in a drizzle. The dog—finally a bit subdued after a visit to the beach for a swim—trotted contentedly. Finn looked out over the gray lake. I followed his gaze and could just barely make out the tiny rock island known as Oodzee-hozo by the Abenaki people, the creator of Lake Champlain at rest and admiring his creation. Finn kept sauntering down the path along the water. At thirteen, he is on a precipice with childhood on one side, something more complex and heavy on the other. His body is lean and kid-like, but the swim team has started to give him solid, rounded shoulders that weren't there a few months ago. He is leaving me, in a way. Packing on muscle for his launch into the world. His orbit grows.

He stands looking out at the waves. His body is always moving, his arms swinging, his hands grabbing branches and leaves. Legs running or kicking, too much energy to stay still. He has so much life it overflows the brim. Coming back to the bike path, he speaks conversationally.

"Dying is probably just like before you were born. You're not even there. It's nothing."

My first thought is, *Shit. I can't do this.* This could be that pivotal moment in his youth where I help him frame the reality of our own mortality. That our lives are finite. That we will, in fact, one day die. What should a father say? How can I give this boy assurances I don't have myself? I say the first words that come to my lips.

"I prefer to think of it as 'the time of no waffles.'"

"What?"

"Dying. It's too weird to think about. Too scary. So I just call it 'the time of no waffles' in my head. Because I don't know what will happen, but I'm pretty sure waffles aren't involved."

I acknowledge it was a lame joke. Not my first, by any stretch. I probably should've been more open instead of deflecting the topic with humor. Been more vulnerable, more accepting of his need to talk about such things. But looking back, I realize two things. First, I was speaking the truth. There are no waffles in death, so it pays to take every chance to eat them while you can. This is just pragmatism. The second realization is that I'm not scared to tell him that *death* is inevitable. I'm scared to tell him that *life* is so, so short, and we seem designed by some perverse logic to never realize how precious the moments are. One minute you're bouncing a baby on your knee, consumed by trying to control the sheer volume of diarrhea and vomit spewing from its orifices every time you try to sit down at a restaurant; the next minute that infant has grown up and is walking away from you down the sidewalk to catch the bus to the mall to meet friends, ingest a billion calories of highly processed fast food, and keep the wheels of the American economy churning by buying cheap plastic crap made in China.

I flash back to a memory of years ago. Finn had been diagnosed with cholesteatoma, a rare ear disease that required multiple surgeries. We took him in early in the morning for the first operation. He played with blocks and tumbled around on a brightly colored mat on the ground while his mom and I sat tensed and worried. Eventually, the surgical team arrived, and I walked with them all to the operating room, dressed in those goofy suits and booties and hair nets to minimize infection. His doctor was there—Dr. Barrington—patiently explaining the procedure to me. She was a small woman, with straight sandy hair tied back in a simple ponytail. She had the most piercing, intense eyes I'd ever seen. I didn't hear a word she said, and could only instead stare at my son, this fragile kid now lying on a hospital gurney. As we talked, the anesthesiologist lowered the mask onto Finn's face, and his eyes slowly closed.

One of the nurses—and holy shit, am I grateful for those humans— led me back out to where Cynthia, my wife, was waiting. I tried to keep my voice steady and calm, told her that Finn looked fine and the doctor said everything was going to be okay. I then went to the bathroom. I shut the door and broke down, great toddler-like sobs coming out of me. I squatted on the floor, chest heaving and my whole body shaking. I don't know if I've ever been so scared in my life. I understood at that moment why events like this drive people to religion. But I didn't believe in anything like that, so I just let loose great racking sobs. I didn't pray to God, but I wished with atomic force that Dr. Barrington had studied hard in med school and had her game face on.

He was fine—if you can call two more surgeries fine—but I couldn't help but dive into the memory of that awful morning even as he stood there in front of me, rain plastering down his hair, grinning and chucking pebbles far out into the lake to watch the splash. I wondered if in my head he'd always be that little kid, defenseless and on a hospital bed, and me standing there useless as life took its course around him.

I don't want to tell him that life can become an endless progression of moments that feel largely meaningless: forty minutes on the phone arguing about a $250 deductible for windshield replacement with some insurance clone; fruitlessly scanning inboxes for messages of good cheer; filling out some endless survey from human resources designed expressly to make you want to eat your own soul. He deserves so much more than that.

He smiles and chuffs a polite laugh at my lame joke as we continue walking. After a few moments he says, "How do you *know* there aren't waffles?"

I smile and raise my eyebrows conspiratorially. I think, *Please let this moment be all moments.* Don't screw this one up. Please let it last. The rain, the lake, the dog. Oodzee-hozo. Walking with him, seeing him strong and healthy, life in front of him. I try to hang on to the feeling.

Acknowledgments

Having a teammate who provides the right mix of encouragement and discipline makes writing a book a bit less of a slog. When I sent my long-suffering editor, Gene Brissie, yet another email intended to dodge and stall on delivering the manuscript, full of promises that I'd "have a draft of the ms to you soon," Gene replied with a single, graceful line: "Define *draft* and *soon*."

Ouch. It was exactly the sort of nudge I needed. So, for that, and countless other moments of support and encouragement, I'm grateful.

Due to my abysmal attendance record as a student and only a passing acquaintance with the rules of the English language, my writing often needs quite a bit of doctoring. Alden Perkins and Ann Seifert triaged my wounded prose to make it better; they have my humble thanks. Big props to all the good people at Globe Pequot and Rowman & Littlefield as well. Takes a crew to bring a book to life. Your efforts are appreciated.

For the cover design, thanks so much to Devin Watson. You captured the cartoonish essence of my life perfectly.

I've often thought of the folks who read early drafts of a book like royal food-tasters. They're willing to take big mouthfuls of meals that may contain poison and kill them, or at the very least give them a regrettable case of diarrhea. And yet they do it, bravely, forgoing their own safety for the good of the reader. These rare souls deserve my thanks: Scott Wurdinger, Gail Storey, John Zecher, Mike Shonstrom, and Teresa Lynn Hasan-Kerr. Special gratitude in this category goes to Hasan-Kerr, who took more time and effort to work through various drafts than any sane human should. I'm so appreciative of her brilliance.

I've had the honor to work in outdoor education on and off for a long time. I'm grateful for every single kid I've had the pleasure to tromp around nature with. Thanks so much to everyone: Outward Bound, Pasadena Waldorf School, Gael Blair Academy, Odyssey Charter School, San Gabriel Mountaineering School, Aurora, Nomad Youth, and Champlain

College. You guys made life a heck of a lot more fun than it would've been without you.

My father, Mike Shonstrom, has gifted me with more outdoor adventures than anyone. He's taken me on so many wild outings, they'd need their own book to recount (like the time he nearly led my fiancé and me into a tornado on a bike ride—remember that one, Dad?). He and my stepmother Amy have my love and gratitude.

I don't know who I'd be without my kids. Except I'd have a lot more money. But their love and laughter keep me going in every part of my life. I love them so damn much sometimes I don't even know how to deal with myself. Vivien and Finn, you two are the center of my world.

And then there's Cynthia, my wife. First reader, best friend, truest heart. Twenty years, and I wouldn't trade a moment. Except maybe the time I tried to cook a whole raw chicken over a campfire in the desert and then had those, er, issues that night in our tent. Sorry about that. Anyway, her love and passions are fierce and burn bright; she's the most fascinating person I've ever met. Can't wait for whatever's coming at us over the horizon.

Finally, *you*, my reader. You've got my book in your hands. Wherever you are, know that you've helped a goon like me achieve a lifelong dream. Thanks.

Index